LETTER MACHINE EDITIONS TUCSON, AZ DENVER, CO

Grace Period

Notebooks, 1998-2007

Grace Period

Notebooks, 1998-2007

Aaron Kunin

Acknowledgments:

Parts of this book first appeared in the following print and online journals: *Black Warrior Review, The Coming Envelope, markszine, Seneca Review, Sonora Review, Trickhouse,* and *Triple Canopy*. "I used to be different. Now I'm the same," "Are we not humane?", and "Still waiting for an apology" were collected in the chapbook *Secret Architecture*, published by Braincase Press. Some of the language and ideas can be found in my other books too.

This book is for David and Rachel.

Published by Letter Machine Editions
Tucson, Arizona 85721

Book Design by HR Hegnauer
Printed in the U.S.A.
Cataloging-in-Publication Data is on file at the Library of Congress

ISBN: 978-0-9887137-0-3

lettermachine.org

Distributed to the trade by Small Press Distribution (spdbooks.org)

Contents

3 What do you do when you're all alone?

17 Won't everything turn out fine (if it turns out the way I want)!

31 Crisis in the American emotions

45 Attacks on style / (proud of your awkward style)

59 "I used to be different. Now I'm the same"

73 A touch of knowledge

85 Red noise

95 Are we not humane?

107 Still waiting for an apology

117 Awkward without w

141 Masculinity is a rare thing

161 Semper Kunin semper pudor

181 The book of which I alone was ashamed

205 Sex and serious

231 The collected lies of AK

255 The world cup for boredom

277 Journal of pleasant studies

291 Merciless fun

301 The better fabricator

What they want is for you to love them, or, failing that, to be thinking about them all the time.

What do you do when you're all alone?

[September 1998-May 1999]

1

Places where I can't write: Minneapolis, Providence, Williamstown, Durham, Baltimore. Anywhere with food, anywhere with books (especially the library). The city, the country. Leaving only: bed.

2

Dream: I hear the word "potica" distinctly spoken in a huge public library. I approach a table where some women are sitting and interrogate them. Which one of them said it? A woman raises her hand. What does it mean to them? Is it an ordinary thing? They're all familiar with it? Have they eaten it or made it? I keep circling the table and asking questions, but they won't tell me what they know.

3

The names of actions.

Being on the make. Making it ("They used to 'make it' under the table in science class"). Making out / passing out. Making a pass.

Making a pass. Passing out ("I passed out"). Passing out forms ("I passed them out yesterday"). Pass / fail. Pass / no pass. Do you have a pass? Horseman, pass by! Passing the drugstore, passing the high school, passing out of high school. Pass on, pass away. "He passed." Coffee? "I'll pass."

4

I have the impression that I know a lot about her, having read what she has read and what she has written.

5

Was I not paying attention when she answered that question, was I still thinking about asking it, or was I thinking that I hadn't asked it yet?
Is that why I can't remember what she said?

6

Do you save everything or do you let it go
I let most everything go
Well if you had something worth saving
I had something and I let it go

7

I always thought that I looked somewhat like her; therefore I hated to hear her looks disparaged.

8

title: "American poets"
I don't think of T.S. Eliot as an American. Not in the way that I think of myself as American.

9

Stephen: "Every English department needs some very smart people and some very nice people."
Which one are you, Stephen? Which one am I?

10

How could you get excited by speeches?

11

There are going to be some long sentences in this book, so we'd better start with some short ones.

12

The problems are psychological as opposed to personal.

13

In this sense even I'm not shy: because "shy" means reluctant to expose yourself, whereas I constantly put myself in positions where I am expected to perform and know that I will not.

14

Failures of taste: Beckett. Antonioni. Shakespeare. The Beatles.

15

Problems in Jabès.

Delusion: "Paris is not my place, my true place."

Mystification: "The book has become my true place."

Fact: Paris, an unfamiliar place, has made him more aware of himself, allows him to recognize aspects of himself (Jewishness) previously unexplored.

In his "true place" he can't think because he can't observe; the place is invisible.

Lie: "Because . . . when two people talk, one of them must always remain silent."

(E.J. lies knowing very well that he is lying)

Fact: two people can talk at once, but writing is no good at representing simultaneous speeches.

This list could be much longer.

16

Graphological portrait.

He often went over letters to add features that hadn't come out clearly on the first pass. This tended to give the letters a worried aspect; there were lines all around them, pouring out of them, and deep creases in the places where the lines joined, as though they had been losing sleep.

The halo of uncertainty around each of your letters.

The mantle of shyness that your writing wears.

"We'll break through this mantle of shyness yet!"

17

Question: how has his writing changed as a result of his new pen (since, after all, all pens really are different)?

—He writes much more slowly; tends to make copying errors (substituting one word for another); ascenders and descenders have a tendency to join in the middle; the writing becomes bigger, rounder, but sometimes lower to the ground, almost a wavy line; takes up more space but may not be easier to read. The new pen may also have affected his spelling.

18

No wonder the characters complain of boredom! He has condemned them to reenact scenes from other stories.

19

He bites the sandwich as though whispering in its ear.

He talks to it in a way that recalls his efforts to amuse his son.

20

How do they know all poetry isn't like this?

21

A quietness that draws attention to itself.

Something about your way of withdrawing asks to be drawn out.

22

There is no room in this workshop for truth.
No membership in literature, no dedication to literature.
Instead, write of the glance.

23

The novel lives over its own cesspool.

24

What's the matter, don't you like your sweet roll?
Don't eat your sweet roll while I'm talking!—a double bind.

25

You sign it "sincerely," but you do not feel at all sincere.

26

People are petty, and people are petty, and pettiness extends in time.
It's the least petty thing.

27

He gives you a marvelous opportunity to examine him when he looks away.

28

"But I don't like men; I like boys."

"There's a difference."

29

Most people, when they want to impress someone, try to conceal their faults, but you magnify them.

30

Afraid that I wouldn't be able to work.

Afraid that I would.

31

Who raised you?

Who revised you?

32

People who know you through someone else don't know what to say when the other person isn't there.

"Where's your friend?" "How is she?"

Like a severed limb.

33

AARON PEELS AN ORANGE VE-RY CAREFULLY.

34

In what terms has he been described?
Why did I think he was American?
(Turning a historical question into a psychological one.)
Why did I think he was drunk?

35

Are the patterns in your relations ones that you choose, are they compulsions, or are they coincidence?

36

You have a sarcastic side.
—Actually I don't. It's because you think I'm more intelligent than I really am. I have to accept the reward of sarcasm or reveal that I was speaking sincerely.

37

When I give something away, I try not to make it into an obligation for the recipient. I usually do this by disparaging the gift. Or else by making the gift part of a series (to diminish its uniqueness).

38

The desire to correct a mistake.
To take the pen out of his hand, turn it around, and write his name for him.

39

You don't know me well enough to make fun of me.

40

He liked to run and leap, so they put him on the playing field.

Systems are on the playing field.

41

How can it be a game if nothing is repeated?

42

Not only all human endeavor. Not only the web of engagements. The most basic activities.

43

They profess to be worried about each other in a way that suggests that each is delighted to see how badly the other is doing.

44

Cognitive portrait.

Her mind, a sharpness that takes the form of confusion.

Sharpen your wits on my confusion.

45

Each one depends on the other person in a conversation to perform the same crucial function to keep it going, so they can't talk to each other.

46

Not a writer but a maker of spectacles.
Are you speaking in lines or sentences and paragraphs? Are you only showing me a picture of speaking?

47

Some people have the right to touch you.

48

Different in many ways, different physically, why would the feeling be the same? How could it be?
What makes you think the feelings are even comparable? Between men and women? One body and another? Between two cities?

49

"I love her breakfast stories" (dream sentence)
"It isn't always something you want to read at the table, though, while you're eating!"

50

An hour later. This time I'm not so happy to be awakened.

51

Because it describes me, I think it belongs to me.

52

I should be afraid of you because there's something menacing, something not very nice, about the wall decorations in your office.

53

The "gift of the magi" is real. It happens all the time: consciously or not, people accommodate one another by exchanging and diminishing the qualities to which they are adapting, until the original qualities are gone, and only the adaptations remain.

54

She demonstrates the thing she doesn't like on you. Using your shoulder.

55

Laughing at him in a way that is almost possessive.

56

Graphological portrait.

Each letter was slightly imperfect and had to be adjusted in order to become legible.

57

If only he could be like a drawing (arrangement of lines and surfaces).

Won't everything turn out fine
(if it turns out the way I want)!

[June-September 1999]

1

My problem is that I don't believe in psychology.
My problem is that I don't see that as a problem.

2

Heightened awareness. Objects that produce this condition.
Does tea heighten awareness?
Does the newspaper?

3

Her confidence in talk. "Everybody knows it because everybody says it."
Couldn't you say: "Nobody knows it because everybody says it."
How well does saying represent knowing?
How else do you elicit what someone knows?

4

I regret my participation in any game.
And I also regret my failure to participate in many games.

5

Prey to old affects. At the mercy of outdated emotions.
I continue to be moved and governed by them.
I no longer feel them, but they regulate my behavior.

6

The cleverness problem.

"Men always prefer the clever woman if she only knows how to use her cleverness." (*Phineas Finn*)

Clever: a way of thinking that can't think about itself.

Clever: knowledge out of control.

7

Smoking: example of complicity between faces and hands.

8

The way she rapped on the side of your head!

How those raps took me!

9

Aaron: short for Erroneous.

10

Things I've done that were motivated by jealousy—conversations, things I've written, attendance at certain events—seem uncharacteristic.

11

How is he going to tell the story of what you have seen? The story you have already heard?

12

Why do you close your eyes and open your mouth?

13

She made the face of a person trying to stifle a cough.

14

There's more than one way of going insane.

15

He has such good taste in everything except food.

16

He thinks a lot more about his involvement with her in her absence, although she claims he does not think about her.

17

There's no room for non sequiturs in this book.

18

Everyone wants this information, but no one wants to pay for it.

19

That's not a button they will want to push a second time.

20

He shifted, wiped his nose, sniffed; the chair groaned; and none of this was intended to express sadness.

21

The center of power is empty.
Arrive at the center of power; find it empty.
“This isn’t, after all, the power I wanted.”
“This doesn’t give me any actual power.”
“Doesn’t anyone wield power? (Who wields this power that I feel?)”

22

Is it impossible for you to receive a degree that your father did not?

23

Not because his father’s life is the pattern for his, but because his father’s life circumscribes his, expresses its limits.

24

He could write because his father could not.
Because the father was a fluent speaker, the son could not talk to save his life.
As though he had inherited nothing from his father.
And had to find a different way to avoid earning a doctorate.

25

He never touches his face.

26

"Just the usual self-doubt."
"You mean doubts about the profession?"
His bewildered response. Because he has never doubted himself.
And he assumes that you identify with your profession.

27

Does self-doubt mean self-worth?

28

His self-doubt shaken.

29

Incapable of breaking up. Incapable of wanting to break up. As though the history of his parents's marriage, their long period of separation, their unusual compromise (living on different floors of the same house) before finally divorcing (but continuing to live in the same neighborhood), then, a few years later, actually trading houses—as though this expressed a limit in his understanding, as though this model of protracted separation was the only one he knew.
And also, without being aware of it, he does something to prevent the other person from breaking up with him.

30

Written like that, the summary gives me so much pleasure that I don't want to develop it into anything.

31

Dog barking in the street sounds exactly like me swallowing gulps of water.

32

I try to read and eat at the same time.

33

Notice how "failure" recurs in his speech.
"A total failure."
"I somehow failed to recognize . . ."
"I failed to remember . . ."
"My failure of understanding . . ."
"My failings as a teacher."
His expressive failures.

34

I don't understand what you're saying.
—What you said doesn't make any sense either.
At least we seem to speak the same language, which neither of us understands.

35

The notion that crap can't recognize itself.
Crap must be innocent.

36

Then I saw that my worry annoyed her.
She didn't like me, my entire manner annoyed her, but she comforted me at least. How touching.

37

A good day for reading to the blind.
A good day for going into hiding.
A good day for seeking asylum in another country.

38

Cognitive portrait.
His mind, a knife that doesn't cut; a knife that spreads.

39

You can't spend your whole life studying other people.

40

The ability to discern and project what someone wants to see in you.
She attributed to herself, perhaps inaccurately, an ability to become what others wanted her to be.

She credited herself with an ability to transform herself into what others saw, perhaps inaccurately, in her.
She could not decide whether to be proud of this ability or ashamed.

41

To see what someone appreciates and enjoys in you. To become only that. To keep it close. To make it your forte.

42

I need to change my list . . .

I want a new list . . .

I want to change everything on my list . . .

43

Those who hate games take them more seriously than those who enjoy them.
(That's why we hate them.)

44

Try to separate the hum of the refrigerator from the hum of the household.

45

Find someone else to practice on!

46

"Listen to yourself"—something I say to others.
Listen to yourself saying, "Listen to yourself."

47

Graphological portrait.
"You've really let your handwriting go."
"It's gotten so much bigger."
"Measure it."
"And it's so relaxed!"

48

They work harder, don't they, at second-rate schools.

49

Someone asks "what are you thinking" because you are obviously thinking something.
Someone asks "what are you thinking" because she already knows what you are thinking.
How can you disguise your thought?

50

Does it make sense to call it hate?

51

Something about you that isn't comfortable with itself. Many things about you that are not comfortable with one another.

52

"He said you were funny last night."
(A reproof: "Why aren't you funny when you're with me?")
"Must have been the water."
Poland water.

53

Something very Jewish was about to happen.
Intertitle: EVERYONE WAS UNEASY, BECAUSE SOMETHING VERY JEWISH WAS ABOUT TO HAPPEN.

54

Occasionally you have to contribute something to the conversation. I guess you were thinking that if you gave at the office you wouldn't have to do it again.
—Uh, no.
For example, last night you contributed, "Thank you."
(dream conversation)

55

Saving American lunches.
—You saved my lunch!

56

You like to imagine that he makes an exception for you, but obviously he does not; the moment you leave the room he starts to exhibit his contempt for you, describing it to someone, repeating the phrases you have just spoken in his presence.
I try to hear what he hears . . . when I talk, I try to imagine what it will sound like in his voice.
I try to hear myself with his contempt . . .

57

Passing from one life into another.
(Bathroom into bedroom.)

58

We all know at least one thing that is quite beyond our experience.

59

Afraid of his power to communicate illness.
(By talking about it, he gave it to someone.)

60

I know you take me seriously, because you make fun of me.

61

Incapable of sleeping past a certain point.

Crisis in the American emotions

[October 1999-March 2000]

1

My absurd habit of putting off things that I know I'll enjoy.
But pleasures associated with food I hardly ever put off.

2

"I have no objection to that"
=
trying to think of an objection

3

You only like the ones that seem invulnerable.
But if they weren't slightly vulnerable, they wouldn't like you.

4

Not all persons are capable of change.

5

Often those who can afford to be gracious are not.
Because those who can afford to be gracious also can afford not to be.
I've often seen him fail to be gracious.
It doesn't even occur to him usually. When he thinks of it, it comes as a nice surprise to him. He had forgotten that he had grace in his arsenal.

6

Those people who look smart were actually very stupid at the time.
History turned their decisions into smart ones.

7

I decided that he wouldn't want me to say anything about his little pain. But he paused before saying goodbye, and the pause made me think, maybe he does want me to say something. I was about to say it, too, when I suddenly understood, he doesn't really want to hear me say it; he only expects me to. So I said goodbye.

8

He expects it, he's waiting for me to say it, he's steeling himself for it.
He thinks I'm going to give him a shot.
He fully expects me to remind him of this pain and is almost pleased to know what's going to happen.
He thinks I'm going to stick a needle in him. And the irritation of not having his expectation confirmed.

9

Bearing the standard of marriage and family (which I misheard as "famine").

10

Cognitive portrait.
Not smart enough to make yourself happy.

11

You deny it because it's true.
—I don't know why I deny it.

12

Will you admit that you are capable of being bored.

13

He is pleased to find his own imperfections in someone else.

14

You only tell him he won't have any trouble because you know he will.

15

Do they relax in their offices?
Do they sleep on the floor? In their chairs? At their desks?

16

He and I know too much about each other for there to be any possibility of a conversation between us.

17

Everything awkward.
Everything awkward that can be done
in an hour
a day
a lifetime
"I want to do everything awkward that can be done"
in a house
in the kitchen

18

I want to fold everything.
I want to fold it so that it can't be unfolded.
(Anything folded can be unfolded; only a cut thing can't be uncut.)

19

Tentatively scheduled.
Provisionally scheduled.
Reluctantly scheduled.
Mysteriously scheduled.
Secretly scheduled.
Thoughtlessly scheduled.
Carelessly scheduled.
Stupidly scheduled.
Miraculously rescheduled.
Inconsiderately canceled.

20

Unscrupulously canceled.
Unsentimentally canceled.
Accidentally (mistakenly) canceled.

21

Cognitive portrait.
Unpacking the accessories of his mind, at first carefully, then hurriedly and haphazardly.

22

"I see that you have contrived to have it postponed once again."

23

Your wish not to be remembered.
"With any luck, no one will remember us."
"With any luck, none of us will remember."

24

An irresponsible cancelation.
An unwarranted cancelation.

25

Cognitive portrait.
His mind charges like a grizzly.

26

Where does a fictional character enjoy privacy?

27

A man sleeping with his hand over his face.

28

Secure in my self-doubt.

29

So disgusted by his failure to sell himself that he developed a sense of integrity and left the gathering.
So disgusted by his failure to get a good price for his integrity that he gathered up his integrity and went home.
So disgusted by the success that others were enjoying that he no longer desired this success for himself.
So disgusted when he saw others imitate him that he longed to be someone else.
So disappointed in himself that he longed for someone to imitate.
So dismayed that at last he returned to the gathering.

30

"God chose half of me (to suffer)"

31

When you want something, you can't imagine that the rest of the world doesn't want it, or do you imagine that you're the only one?

You cling to the belief that you are ordinary. That there are some others like you.

32

We don't always lie from bad motives.

33

He goes through his own pockets.

34

Difficulty of walking with another person.

Composing the gait.

They could not cross the street together.

They should not have tried.

35

Those who were happy to see him go did not attend the farewell brunch.

36

You're a smile without a mouth.

The eye smiles, the nose smiles, the forehead smiles.

37

They put something in it to keep it from smiling.

38

Actions directed against something invisible.

39

Delighted that no one remembers me.

40

Three things that help:
intelligence
imagination
sense of humor
—But NOT NECESSARY for having successful career as artist. NOT NECESSARY for producing art.

41

Cognitive portrait.
A highly expressive face that gives a misleading impression of thought.
Thoughtful looks; the thoughts are empty.

42

You can't seduce someone with gingerbread.
Gingerbread is only a pretext.

43

A bird revolving around its violated nest.

44

Ideas tend to disappear while grooming, cleaning.
Washing out ideas—

45

Does a chair sit or stand?

46

"My students never understand me. Why would I want to have sex with them?"

47

Is it because you don't want to answer their questions?
Is it because you don't want to know more than they do?

48

My assumption, despite all evidence to the contrary, has been that I am normal.
I remain convinced that others think the way I do.

49

He almost had a cigarette in his mouth.

50

Open your eyes, open your mouth.

51

A sissy, and, at the same time, a bully.

52

How together I look and how not-together you look.
How we look together.
How we look as though we are together.

53

When I sit on a chair, I don't have to know its history.

54

Teach an umbrella how to read.
Teach a pencil how to read.
Teach a chair how to read (a newspaper).
"Reading group" (title)

55

The chair can't read, but it's involved in reading.

56

He was obviously delighted by the possibility that I had been lying to him. That I deliberately invented the story out of nothing.
Savoring it: "Maybe EVERYTHING he tells us is a lie!"

57

Is boredom part of a continuum that includes sleep.

58

If you can understand me, then it's a lie I'm telling you.
If you think you understand, then I'm hiding something.

59

The way he showed that he was out of place.
Uncertain of himself until he knew where you were. Unwilling to put down his coat. Unwilling to have someone take it until you took it from him.
The way he immersed himself in your conversation.
If you had seen that, you would have been pleased.
—But what I saw instead was something that did not please me particularly.

60

“splendidly perverse” (title)

That doesn’t make sense, so why don’t we do that.

Since no one is going to enjoy this, let’s see how much we can increase our discomfort.

Let’s try to make this as weird as possible.

61

Dream sentence: “Remember that nothing worthwhile ever came from cleverness.” It sounds like a warning, but perhaps it was a consolation.

I write down everything he says, apparently forgetting that you can’t carry a piece of paper out of a dream.

Attacks on style
(proud of your awkward style)

[March-December 2000]

1

Why should he do any work?
He has everything he needs.

2

He thoroughly enjoys (appreciates) his own writing.
He finds that they are admirably clear.

3

How well he understands his own thinking.

4

Something to make your self-image manifest in your appearance to others.
Or an event confirms someone's impression of you.

5

Water damage.
While you sleep, the wall bubbles.

6

She would be political in the same unthinking way that she's apolitical.

7

You sold me my orange juice this morning.
. . . was it only this morning?

8

Have you already forgotten your despair of this morning?

9

He regarded himself with interest (interest as a way of disclaiming responsibility).
He regarded himself as though hearing someone give a lecture.

10

Give me a category, I complained.
Give me a category, he demanded.

11

They adhere to their old prejudices in the name of rationality and science.
They use science to confirm their ancient prejudices.
They use science to explain to their children an idea founded on prejudice.

12

Which one do I want? Or do I have the power to make a decision?
Which one am I allowed to want?

13

Graphological portrait.
A particularly ugly capital I.

14

My teachers were indulgent of the chaos of my thoughts.
(Luckily?)
Would it have been better if they had held me to a standard that I could not recognize (or value)?
—Better to preserve your thoughts in their original chaos.

15

"Shy" is always a self-description.
Proof: no one ever sees shyness; they see rudeness, self-absorption, etc.
But they can feel shy, call themselves shy—obviously a device or delusion.

16

How well he appreciates his own writing.
He understands almost every word.

17

She takes no pleasure in food.
She would forget to eat.
(What does she put in?—crackers and peanut butter.)

18

To make art out of dissolute living.

19

They build systems to confirm their prejudices.

20

Your unsuckable thumb.

21

"We proudly serve . . ."

22

It's your own fault: if you're going to be embarrassed by it, you shouldn't keep writing that sentence.

A sentence you would prefer to bury.

23

Men treat her badly because they know she expects it; women treat her badly because they know she won't see it.

She called you a woman—as a compliment—because she was blind to you in the way that she's blind to what women are capable of.

(By her definition, strictly speaking, there was no such thing as a woman.)

Not flattering to be called a woman by her.

24

Universal motto: BUILDING COMPLICATED MACHINES TO CONFIRM YOUR PREJUDICES.

25

"You're marginalizing yourself."
"I don't need to do it myself; I have others to do it for me."

26

Apologizing as a way of repeating the offense.
Or making it worse.
"I don't accept your apology"
"I apologize for my apology"
"For the tone of my apology"

27

On the bus going home he remembered this.

28

She has no power.
She has power only when you give it to her. But she doesn't know what to do with it.
So effectively she still has no power.

29

What are you supposed to do with someone who doesn't even know how to use her power to give you what you want?

30

"I'm not going to let you forget that I'm doing this only to oblige you."

31

You can attack her only because she exists.
Incapable of defending herself only because she exists.
She can defend herself only by ceasing to exist.
"My answer is that I'm already dead."

32

Every time I went to see him, he mistook me for someone else. (He always remembered me, but he remembered me as someone else.)
"Oh yes, you're that actor."
"We were going to work on that screenplay?"
He was inviting me to become more interesting.

33

—Poets of your generation whose writing is suggestive of hidden trauma (I don't include you in this; your trauma is on the surface).

34

You were never my student.
Kissing me you were no longer my student.
"Anyone who kisses me here has not resigned."

35

The bad student is the one who remains a student.

36

Reading them over and over again, do we become more like them?
When they no longer surprise us, are we more like them?

37

The department chair is a chair that sits on you.

38

"I'll never read this book! How interesting!"
Your affection for the books you won't read, don't want to read, managed to avoid reading.

39

"Here's a book I should have read at a different time in my life."

40

You've done enough. Try again tomorrow.

41

There is no English department.
It doesn't exist.
It's a myth.
—Doesn't Harvard have an English department?
Are you kidding? Harvard isn't even a school; it's only a library.
Only the library exists . . .
Nothing there but a library.

42

And we brought the adventure to a conclusion of our own choosing.

43

It's the only thing that keeps me from liking you (if you would just stop doing that, I'm sure I'd like you!).

44

This book shows no sign of having been read by anyone.
But the cover lifts slightly.

45

Difficulty saying certain names, such as your own name.
Difficulty beginning it. A pause at the first syllable.
Difficulty saying it loud enough for anyone to hear.

46

Take my advice!
—Are you advising me to take your advice?
—On what advice do I take your advice?

47

The novel doesn't include this.
You have to look for it somewhere else.
(Maybe the newspaper?)
—Not there either.
Loud music includes this.

48

It's like keeping time with something else that's going on.
It's like something extra inside you that needs to find release through your hand.

49

Because she doesn't speak any foreign language fluently, she ascribes a special significance to foreign words; she allows them to mean something in addition to what they actually mean.

50

His speech doesn't go very far (it seems to trail off but it really just ends).

51

"I almost didn't recognize you."
"I'll take that as a compliment."

52

It's not so hard to get people to say they want to die; we say it all the time.

53

Is that what you were trying to tell me all this time?
Is that why you kept calling?

54

At the start of the conversation, she produces the reason she will give at the end for ending it.

55

"Building new equipment to confirm your inherited prejudices!"

56

A woman is striking the camera.
The camera falls to the ground and she takes its wallet.

57

You notice I'm getting better—you don't notice, but I am getting better.
I don't notice that you don't notice.
Getting better at not noticing.

58

My relationship with them is that I do something wonderful which they fail to understand.

59

Yawns into his hand, then pats his thigh (to stamp out the yawn?).

60

His lips moving too quickly (when he's talking) sometimes accidentally make a kissing sound.

61

I'm buzzing you in.
I'm buzzing you up.

62

It sounds as though I'm talking but I'm actually reading.

63

Disappointment and relief.

64

Comment.

65

But mostly disappointment.

66

Active dislike and sabotage presenting themselves as concern.

67

Coarse behavior / refined perception.

Those who behave without apparent sensitivity are often sensitive to nuances of behavior in others.

68

You get credit for having the thought even if you don't carry it out. Both the part of you that has the thought and the part that represses it are admirable.

69

Reading as decapitation.

"I used to be different. Now I'm the same"

[December 2000-January 2001]

1

The first word is “although.”

2

Not a strong enough advocate of your desire?

3

I think there’s some value to taking everything personally.

4

I want to hurt you; it hurts me that you’re not hurt.
—It hurts me that you’re hurt; I didn’t intend that.
It hurts me that you didn’t intend to hurt me.

5

For spite, I’ll never stop loving you.
As an act of pure meanness, I’ll never stop loving you.
Just to be selfish, I’ll never stop loving you.
Just to be sick, I’ll never recover.

6

The hum of the fish tank kept him awake, so he got up in the middle of the night to turn it off.
The glow of the fish tank, placed directly behind the sofa, made it impossible to sleep, so he reached out pettishly in a fit of half-sleep and turned it off.

The fish boiled in their tank, someone having (maliciously or accidentally?) turned the temperature dial as high as it would go during the night.

7

Headline: STILL WAITING FOR AN APOLOGY.

—Who isn't waiting for an apology? I'm waiting for several apologies . . .

—I stopped waiting for an apology long ago.

8

He would tell you himself if you talked to him for as long as fifteen minutes; you wouldn't have to ask directly . . .

9

You don't deserve a better notebook if you're only going to contaminate it with that deplorable handwriting.

10

Weak tea, strong opinions; and the reverse.

Matching tea with opinions.

11

"For sheer spite, I'm giving up looking after my career."

"Out of generosity, I'm looking after my own interests."

12

"Turns out to be," as though surprise was still possible.
"Turns out to be," as though it was not a foregone conclusion?

13

"You're a very capable person" (capable of what?).

14

She removes something from his pocket and shows it to him. "What's this?"

15

Leaning against the wall justifying his actions.
Unable to sleep until he had accounted for his actions (to himself).

16

Forceful. Discovering what you want to say through force.

17

Why do you remind me that I'm doing you a favor?
To substitute for a power you can't give (the power to be hurt)?
("A very capable person": capable of inflicting pain? Capable of suffering?)

18

When they use the same expressions, you remember that they had once been friends; you wonder if one of them originated it.

19

What do you keep in there?
What do you keep in that big head?

20

Indiscriminate killing. Indiscriminate reading.

21

He noted the danger but did not avoid it.
He noted the danger and then ceased to think about it.

22

I'm glad for you, I'm glass for you.

23

Couldn't think of anything to say that would not extend the conversation.
His silence extended the conversation.

24

She prefers to separate the parts of her life. In anyone else it would be the sign of a moral lapse. Duplicity. (What does she think they might learn from one another if she brought them together, or if they fell into one another's company by chance?)

25

Turning over and rolling out the same ball of dough all afternoon.

26

Graphological portrait.
The shameful mass of your handwriting.
Confronted by your shameful handwriting.
Lines of your handwriting closing on themselves.
An eye turned inward (the shameful mass behind the eyes).

27

Very infrequent occasions when you see that it would be possible to carry yourself differently. "Maybe it would be easier if I believed this; maybe it would be easier to appreciate this than to dislike it; maybe it would be easier to maintain the opposite, etc."

28

And I didn't want to write to you because everything I had to say would have been this . . .

29

Find something to be enjoyed in the interior of the body.

30

I said it and immediately felt that someone in the room disagreed with me (but could not pinpoint the location of the disagreement).

31

The gods, incapable of action because bound to honor their ancient contracts, create human agents to fulfill their obligations and to be free of them; the human surrogates swiftly render themselves incapable of action by creating new contracts to which they are bound.

32

Forced himself to eat, after his lunch, a carrot; ate too quickly, started to choke.

33

Try not to alter the essential character of the place.

34

I was never here.

35

"I'm glad you got what you wanted";
"I can see why you would like that"
=
"You're different from me, and you're predictable"

36

Take what you need (but try not to take more than you need).

37

"Simply being human isn't enough."
You get very little credit for that.

38

I devised this episode to improve the writing in your notebook.

39

"Anyone who wrote such a weird letter would have been trying to communicate something!"

40

Why does it seem degrading to take the chemical in its pure form rather than drowning it in a medium?

41

Resolution that persons from different parts of her life should be kept apart.
Discovery that they could not be separated fully, even in herself: one could not be used as a refuge from the other, or to counteract the other.
Further discovery that mixing them did not increase the pleasure they afforded individually, but only heightened the discomfort and pain they were capable of inflicting.
Any burden imposed by one made the other seem equally demanding; it became necessary to escape from both.

42

Headshake. Handshake.
Head and hand combinations.
The end of his sleeve caught in the handshake.

43

An odd series of manual accidents hindered and deformed the shape of that word.

44

Graphological portrait.
As a result of conscious effort over several months I now automatically make an F whose shape pleases me. But it may not be easier to identify than the old one; it sometimes has the disadvantage of being indistinguishable from T.

45

"What is unforgivable is having the power to forgive and not forgiving."

46

The brightness of your answer is an insult.

Your answer is an insult because it doesn't remember that we've been through this before; because it doesn't remember that this would have been our third attempt, not our second; because it remembers the canceled meeting and forgets the meeting that took place.

47

The cheerfulness of your answer is an insult.

Because a test means something different when the person being tested has already failed.

48

To pretend not to know something that I've told you is an insult.

It is an insult to go on ignoring it after I've given you permission not to ignore it.

49

an insult

A crime demands forgiveness; to demand forgiveness is a crime.

50

It is an insult to forgive me when I've done nothing wrong.
To forgive a person who has no need for forgiveness is an insult.
Those who claim the power of forgiveness: to claim that power and not to exercise it is an insult; exercising it may also be an insult.

51

You forgive me to remind me that I haven't apologized.
"Forgive them for what they do, for they know not what they do; do not forgive them for not knowing."
The demand for forgiveness diminishes the power to forgive; the demand for an apology diminishes the force of the apology.

52

"Could have slept with anyone there."
—Did you make this announcement hoping to have a similar effect on me? (Enjoying the "could have" more than the "slept with.")
"But I don't want to sleep with anyone."
"And I chose this one."
"You've become the only person in the world I don't want to have sex with."

53

Tolerance-irritation, confidence: aesthetic principles.

54

Process laid bare.

55

"I almost lost a year!"

"Maybe the only way to benefit from that year was to lose it."

56

"I was afraid of that," which means I wanted it.

A touch of knowledge

[January-May 2001]

1

Always blame the text, since that's the only part you control.
Or else blame your intention.
(good luck controlling your intention)

2

Unaware of time's passage while washing.

3

Brought up to deplore his lack of spiritual upbringing.

4

Make your self-image manifest in one place.
Or an event confirms someone's opinion of you.
"I dropped the cake!"
Just as you thought.

5

Leave the room so I can think about you.
My supposed inability to leave.

6

What has deformed your English?

7

You asked if I was all right and, when I started to answer, complained that I was keeping you on the phone; that was badly done.

8

He believes that people are capable of believing almost anything, only they're not capable of making more than a few arguments. Perhaps no more than two.
He doesn't hear them say what he doesn't expect.
He congratulates himself because he is able to predict what they will say.

9

I don't think my unconscious knows the geography well enough to direct me to that place.
The fold in the city. "I live at the fold."

10

"You should value yourself more."
Is that how I show that I value myself? By relinquishing what I value?

11

They'll have to catch up; they never will if they don't try, and they won't.

12

Adults will laugh at anything.

13

"I'm doing something inhuman, but the action is accompanied by an unpleasant feeling that reminds me I'm human."

14

Always tired, half-asleep, not receiving the customary benefit from sleep (the benefit of sleep is waking).

15

He knew very well that he was dealing with an extraordinary individual and did not particularly want to be dealing with him.

16

Permission to stare at someone for an hour.

17

And then you got that ridiculous award, which you knew didn't mean anything; nonetheless it changed you; I don't respect you.

18

Sixty cups of tea later . . . "You're absolutely nothing to me."

19

Perfected. Perfected out of existence.

20

Words, go together
Protect me, umbrella, once more
Care for me, book, again
Support me, chair, again

21

I noticed that you felt more comfortable in the presence of another person, and that the other person also noticed and was made uncomfortable by this, or by my distress.

22

Banging head against light fixture you unfortunately grunted (you despise yourself for grunting, for not suppressing it) but at least didn't put hand on head.

23

A touch of knowledge.
Part of the trouble with him is that he isn't wrong about everything, but what he knows is inevitably deformed by his personality.

24

"We prefer to exist as examples."

25

When he calls he says it's quarter after seven because he's been thinking about calling since that time.

26

When he calls he says it's quarter after seven because he promised himself he wouldn't call until then.

27

With some people their lateness is expected; with others it should be expected but never fails to surprise.

28

They do it with bits and pieces of useless information, which they collect. "Touches" of knowledge.
They do it with nothing. A "vacuum system." A void whose emptiness you have to maintain.
You have to isolate the thought from the impurities of its atmosphere—its naturally impure environment.

29

Your handwriting changes after you've spoken.

30

And you are forced to think about it.

31

"This." Holding it up for inspection.

32

At least half of style is compulsive.

33

"These books have gotten more interesting."

34

Words suggesting themselves, he looked for an occasion to say them.

35

arouse
Your insecurities amuse me.

36

She whispers an unnecessary apology, making its acknowledgment necessary.

37

Some who don't read books are very interested in the contents of books; some know what's inside them without appearing to read them.

38

How many times a day do you want to show your tongue?

39

Surprised into telling the truth. Protecting one truth, you inadvertently reveal another.

40

He gave the order; its enactment surprises him (by then he's forgotten).

41

Prize student and problem student.
Prize and problem. Never student.

42

"You have perfectly grasped the point of my book."

43

Your pride is easily overcome.
It's not your pride that keeps you from getting what you want.

44

An unusual case of someone who lost her sense of humor. More frequently it develops over time.

45

You are not improved by being rained on.

46

Magnifying glass on the desk. "I need it to read poetry."

47

The verbal equivalent of a shrug.

48

Sheet of paper passed around the room until it reaches the person to whom it is addressed. Forcing that person to leave the room.

49

The frowning head on the molasses cookie.

50

Because we don't know where thought takes place, we can put it anywhere.

51

Inventing new words to characterize the utter superficiality of Alan's project.
He came out of retirement to write a negative review of Alan's book.
He came out of retirement in recognition of the superhuman frailty of Alan's book.

52

Stirs; swallows. "Take note of those stirs." "Take note of those swallows."

53

Changing orientation to get a complete picture.
The direction of your sleep.
—You've straightened my rest!

54

Purifying stares. "Your gaze purified me."

55

The side of the Copperfield truck "has eyes but cannot see."

56

He only responds to those who don't understand him (a Christian model of explanation).

57

No, she didn't get "what she wanted."

Only, out of the choices available to her, she got the one she picked.

58

It embodies everything about him that's rotten; fortunately it's just a piece of writing.

59

A novel expresses a deficiency.

Red noise

[May-August 2001]

1

No chance that his life will ever be more complicated than it is now (not because a more complicated life can't be imagined, not because a more complicated life can't be assigned to him; simply because he lacks the technology to handle complications: without that technology, life remains simple).

2

As though life automatically became more complicated in stages ("I can't wait" until your life becomes this complicated).

3

Difficulty counting on fingers because they're more strongly identified with letters than numbers.

4

The only one who gets it right: therefore, without interest. The solution is without interest.

5

Demanding assent: therefore, not a sincere question.

6

inert writing, inert wording
incapable writing, incapable of writing

7

The terrible secret is that no food tastes good at this height.

8

The habit of writing in books, encouraged in schools.

9

Leaving a puzzle to be solved later.
At a lower height where objects of interest are created, and appetites aroused.

10

"My dad has a coat just like that and it frightens me to see you in it."

11

Dinner was delivered to the wrong house.

12

You taste different.
—Different from how I used to be or from what you're used to?

13

"I'll just have an empty cup."

14

Funloving, unloving.

15

Puts his hand on top of his head to keep from stabbing himself in the eye.

16

Both sides acting in bad faith for their mutual benefit. They don't recognize mutual benefit as a possibility.

17

Every English department is unhappy in its own way.

18

Tendency to confuse self-promotion with education: therefore, ineffectual publicists.

Whenever anyone offers you something they value, take it! (The goal of publicity is not to make yourself understood as you wish to be understood, but to discern and project whatever they want to see in you.)

19

"Much as I admire him, I don't want to be associated with him."

20

"I trust you because I know you'll never write about me."

21

No living thing could survive for long in your notebook.
—There are many living things in my notebook.

22

Your notebook is unhygienic.

23

Feelings are always mutual.

24

Again he wrote the heading "Psychoanalysis of the classroom" and wrote nothing under the heading.

25

Graphological portrait.
Bizarre shapes of your letters—ratty, shaggy letters.
Your letters shedding their skins.

26

You don't want to know what's happening in your apartment while you're showering.
He unfortunately stepped out of the shower too early.

27

Sometimes you have the same idea more than once.
Different circumstances inspire the same idea.

28

Not how you wish to be understood but perhaps how you wish. Not what you meant but perhaps what you wanted.

29

Still, unfortunately, legible.

30

He tries to eat lunch while his body, still under the spell of the machine it has been working, continues to perform its mechanical task.

31

If this space were wider it could be traversed faster (you would take full steps).

32

If you're going to continue making your noise, I might as well start making my noise.

33

The fact that you can argue something convincingly is a fact about you, not the argument or the thing you are discussing.

34

Your speech becomes highly idiomatic on the phone and in moments of arousal.

35

It's amazing how many people, if you ask what they want, will say they don't know.

(Not because they don't know. Because they believe that saying it won't help them get it.)

36

They endeavor to hide their ambitions, even when, which happens occasionally, they are asked to disclose them, for fear that premature disclosure of an ambition would prevent its achievement, either because talking about it might make it available to another ambitious person who's in a better position to succeed with it, or because someone in a position to prevent the achievement might be horrified by the extent of the ambition. Unfortunately nothing is more difficult to keep to oneself than a strong ambition.

37

Only the wording did not return.

38

In place of a tail.

No mane, no tail: where do you grip him?

39

You want them to understand your position; you don't care if they come around to it.

40

Haven't you ever excused yourself from the table in order to write something in privacy?

41

Trying to predict where the phrase will recur in his memory. Trying to create conditions in which it will recur.

42

I was almost a little embarrassed because I'd been so nice; they were certainly embarrassed by my grotesque performance.

43

You get better reception while walking.

44

This theater is not cold enough.
This theater is warm enough to support life; cool it down.
This theater doesn't kill fast enough; it lets you escape before killing you.
The kind of laughter the world needs.
Cold laughter. Cold enough to kill.

45

They would bring *Capital* to a desert island.

46

Another thing I don't want to be associated with.

—But if you have to be associated with it (distasteful thought), what are the benefits?

47

If the person approaches from the wrong angle, greeting is impossible.

48

Her efforts to help invariably fail, perhaps because her intentions are not, in reality, particularly generous.

Are we not humane?

[August 2001-January 2002]

1

Perhaps this is some kind of holiday?

2

People look for the same things in different places.

3

He read blunderingly, as though he had wandered into a fight involving a lot of people.
He read brutally, as though trying to extract information from a suspect.

4

You feel as though you're doing them a tremendous favor, although they did not ask for your help and seemed to be getting along quite well without you.

5

Chosen cares. Created cares.
"I can only care about artificial things."

6

All of my essays have at least two beginnings.
—Your head has at least two openings.

7

His speech was increasingly addressed to inanimate objects.

8

They had what they later described as a lively discussion.

9

Offended by their tact.

10

The necessity of skipping a space (skipping over the words that would be printed in that space).

11

Food rather than art.

12

He's making my slips for me.
But he knows they're my slips not his.

13

Yes. I should probably think about it first, but yes.
The answer will be yes.

14

I'm giving you this information because I firmly believe that you will not know how to use it.

15

Unfair to ask if the person can't say no.

16

Reviews.

"I can't tell from your reviews whether you like the person or not."

"I can't tell from your reviews whether you read the book or not."

"I can't tell from your reviews whether you speak English or not."

17

The bat plate.

One worries about squashing the bat under the plate; one is also, perhaps, a little threatened by the bat.

18

Such ingratitude! After all I've done for you—things you don't even know about . . .

—I can hardly be grateful for things I don't know about.

19

My small contribution to dinner.

20

That word is exerting a subtle pressure on the rest of the sentence, and perhaps on the preceding sentence.

21

Familiar only with the collections in which his own work appears.
A poem "appears."
—It appears to be a poem.

22

Unable to sense awkwardness.
Good manners are coextensive with a capacity for awkwardness.

23

Because she is insensitive even to the most blatant awkwardness, any situation is acceptable to her in which her desires have been fulfilled. The manner of their fulfillment makes no difference.

24

Their success is hardly evidence of intelligence or foresight.

25

The backpack crawls on its belly like a spider.

26

There's no reason to suppose that using words makes you smarter.

27

"Now they're all going to forget about me."

"No one's going to buy my book."

"Rotten luck."

"Too bad his book had to come out immediately before a terrorist attack."

"This is really going to hurt sales of my book."

28

Uses a political crisis to extend his vacation and enhance his personal comforts.

29

This man died of criticism.

30

Art is not on the side of other art.

31

The tendency to produce assenting expressions.

32

To ask "whether this person will be helpful" of everyone you encounter does not help.

33

"I'm calling every number in this book because I don't remember who any of these people are."

34

Your gestures gave a more accurate description than your speech.

35

So sad, but not nearly as sad as everything else.

36

Headline: STILL NO PUBLISHER FOR ARTICLE.

37

This pen makes less noise.
This poem has a word in it.

38

A mouth accustomed to forming the words.

39

Bred for color and sound (or "bite")—not texture or shadow.

40

That person is a white lie.
That person is a prophylactic.

41

—Not sad enough. Still too amusing.

42

Confidential memorandum.
Heading: OF NO CONCEIVABLE INTEREST TO ANYONE OUTSIDE OF ITS COMMUNITY.

43

Eyes closed. Taking large bites. Chewing meditatively.

44

Aren't you afraid that this cheap hotel pen is going to corrupt your writing?

45

As I sign my name it appears on my face in glowing letters.

46

He writes his name in one place and it appears in another place.

47

He knocks on the door and another door opens.

48

Most do not find the sleep of the dead so refreshing.

49

His hands around his *own* neck.

50

As with many other problems, I want to blame her influence but am not sufficiently familiar with her work.

51

He makes circular gestures to ask for a pen.
He points to his hand to ask for a pen.
Then he points to the surface he is going to write on.

52

He is apparently more familiar with their arguments than they are.

53

He puts no value on writing—look at his pen for god's sake!

54

Uncanny ability to say the same thing every time as though discovering it for the first time.

55

His forehead ached from holding up the eyebrows.
Straining to keep up its characteristic expression of surprise.

56

"More than you wanted to know"

=

"I have calculated exactly how much you want to know, and I'm telling you more anyway"

A coarse remark based on sensitivity.

57

They would never say it was too good for them.

58

Deprived of sleep you also lack a conscience.

59

An example of food poisoning.

Another way of practicing non-intentionality.

60

Sensitive to all awkwardness but powerless to remove it.

Too embarrassed to acknowledge it.

61

Their only way of having authority in our culture is through the sinecures they deny themselves and begrudge one another.

62

Extended wear by turning inside out.

Wore all her clean clothes and wore them a second time inside out; wore all her roommate's clean clothes and wore them a second time inside out . . .

63

Notice: NO BOOKS WILL BE PERMITTED IN THIS RESTAURANT.

64

Occasional contact with artifacts from a primordial moment in the history of the personality—e.g., "my favorite book" only in the sense that it could not be replaced by anything and at a certain level you are still the same person.

65

Notice: IF YOU HAVE NO BOOK, ONE WILL BE PROVIDED BY THE RESTAURANT.

66

Another potluck.

"Even entertaining you they want to get something out of you."

Still waiting for an apology

[February-May 2002]

1

Too poor to afford a xerox, he memorized the quotation.
—He couldn't copy it by hand? Could he not afford a pencil? Wasn't he really making a spectacle of his poverty? His memory?

2

He takes me seriously and believes I always tell the truth, so I should be careful what I say to him.

3

At a certain point the word "between" disappears.
First the quotation marks disappear.

4

We've got to keep that unpronounceable name alive!
We've got to extend the use of that unpronounceable name!

5

Whether to diminish suffering or enjoy the satisfaction of keeping to yourself a technique for diminishing suffering.

6

Conspicuously absent: in order to create a situation in which everyone would be talking about him.

7

Everyone else uses that phrase; I have never used it.

8

We're not having the conversation I envisioned and rehearsed; we're having the conversation you envisioned and rehearsed.

9

His explanation has been disproved, but he still offers it and does not search for another.

10

She gets a little closer to volunteering personal information in saying that she will not do it.

11

Their behavior appears inexplicable if you forget they're trying to tell a story.

12

This cigarette has a riddle in it.
This cigarette has a lie in it.

13

They would ask: "Is it allowed?"

14

It has flavor because it suffers.

—What, you're going to decide this based on taste?

15

In some cases, their imagination is shaped by what they want; in some cases, they have no imagination.

16

Every time she started to say something, he murmured, "Uh-huh."

17

She thinks she understands: "Oh."

She really gets it: "Oh."

18

News about a non-event travels even faster.

19

My name did not seem to surprise you.

20

Close your eyes in front of books and paintings.

21

You could hear their separate laughs.

22

. . . "bald" which could mean at least five different things; "completely bald" which could mean the same number of things.

23

Everyone draws in air as though about to laugh.

24

She creates new contracts, binds herself to them, releases herself from them, and feels better.
An effective therapy for mild depression.

25

The inside of your body doesn't look like a diagram.

26

I don't want to be too consistent or too painstaking but in spite of myself I am.

27

Here I am using a word I would never use.

28

"You've got a big shield."

29

Collaboration on injury.

Through my relaxed attitude toward your strict policy, we create suffering.

30

Anticipation kept me awake; now fulfillment is putting me to sleep.

Awareness erupts "through chinks that time has made."

31

The other half is reflective.

The first half is compulsive.

32

"Dry toast"

Those who attend lectures for the promise of food afterwards.

Those who cater lectures as a pretext for attending them.

33

Graphological portrait.

Holding the pen as you would hold a cigarette—from the base, close to where you would put your mouth.

34

An anvilist.

"dropping another anvil on an unsuspecting public"

35

They are known and published by one another.

36

"You live by your taste."

37

Because she tells people everything but doesn't get everything right.

38

"Then I can be human."

"Is that all that's keeping you from being human?"

39

The moment when he discovered that he was better than everyone else occurred at a party in the sixties.

40

With a knife, he crossed out the name TESS where it once appeared on the barrel of the pen; he then used the pen to inscribe the name TESS on the handle of the knife.

41

It's a bit like trying to figure out if you're wearing glasses or not.

42

The lies they tell are more reasonable than their truths. Reason gets in the way of their effort to tell the truth.

43

"Why didn't he assume I was lying? He's clearly lying all the time—I assume."

44

His clunky lying.

His lying is distinguished by the noise it makes when it strikes the floor.

45

Proudly: "And I didn't lie."

46

In a program like this no one is going to have a finished piece, not even you, or, one might say, least of all you, but yours is the only one that looks finished.

47

Their only ambition as writers is to write a lot.

48

His only topic of conversation is previous conversations with more interesting people than you.

49

"I thought I'd find you here."

"At a lecture I'm giving?"

"Speakers don't always show up for their own lectures."

50

Pretend ignorance—that usually works.

Although it's mortifying.

51

My job is to apologize for those who previously held my job.

52

"Employees are not able to accept compliments."

53

Worried that in a late stage of senile forgetfulness, or perhaps in only ten years, as a result of some revolution in his intellectual development, he would no longer recognize the quotation.

54

A recurring dream—no, he just keeps talking about it.

55

My name doesn't look like me, but it sounds like me.

56

There is nothing wrong with being *tainted*.

Awkward without w

[May-October 2002]

1

May your hands be too big for your pockets.

2

I am not threatened by it because it is not trying to depict me.

3

It had been cooked in water, and was served with water.

4

Not merely convenient forgetfulness, because sometimes her forgetfulness benefits others, sometimes herself; in this case herself.

Indiscriminate, sincere forgetfulness.

5

They make no distinction between their important achievements and insignificant or forgettable ones.

"Did you see my interview?" (a complete puff piece)

"I won my squash game."

6

Ostentatiously she removes her glasses from the glittering case and sets them on her nose, deferring the moment when she will look through them.

7

"I had a dream about you in which you did not appear." Alarming: because the fantasy is operating as interpretation.

8

He'll give it to anyone who asks for it, even if they don't mean it.

9

Do you take unsigned checks?
Do you take out-of-state third-party checks?

10

"We don't applaud."

11

When they really care about something they stop working.

12

One of those gestures a society makes toward things it doesn't value but pretends to.

13

We always defy our gods.

14

I assure you, she's really famous.

15

Both aggressively infantile and aggressively maternal.

16

He laughs politely and impolitely—in short at every opportunity.

17

I feel a bit odd with them because they're never laughing. Whereas I'm in the habit of laughing, wanting to laugh, on the verge of laughter, all the time.

18

The first step in taking someone's wallet is figuring out where it is (seeing him put it in his pocket, for example); before that, figuring out if there's anything in it worth taking.

19

You won't understand.
—Not if you say it like that.

20

If you want him to desire something, you shouldn't apologize for it.
The best way for him to desire something is to trick him into believing that he's fulfilling your desire.

21

Why are we friends? We're not friends; you just recognize me.

22

They complain that the scene is dead there, which may mean simply that no one was sufficiently eager to welcome them on their return.

23

They grab each other because they're feeling drawn to other people.

24

He can only write intelligible sentences.

25

Not all awkwardness has two Ws.

26

The only way they have of getting back at you is telling the truth, so you're safe.

27

Haven't seen you in a while.

—I stopped buying from you when you recognized me.

28

“Uniquely compassionate”—i.e., in a way that no one else would understand as compassionate.

29

Overslept: you’re having the same dreams you had earlier in the evening.

30

What made him think the phone was ringing?
He often picked up the phone and spoke a tentative greeting into it, as though he suspected that it was trying to ring. Or suppressing a ring—someone was trying to reach him.

31

If other boys could speak, they would say the same thing.

32

One of the things his writing looks for is comfort. It finds it.

33

Anxiously feeling the outside of his pocket for an object that should have been in it.

34

If the idea is unfinished or simply wrong, I don’t like to say it, but sometimes I will say it so as not to be silent.

35

Graphological portrait.
The signature of someone who isn't often asked to sign his name.

36

I remain loyal to your former dislike.
I continue to treat that person as though you don't like her.

37

If they only know one thing about it, they feel compelled to say it.
They have to show how little they know to keep the conversation going.

38

Thus, theory is a way for crude intellects to enjoy the benefits of sensitivity.
Thus, sensitivity can be replaced.

39

My sleep had no character.

40

Not quite as dumb as he'd planned to be.

41

He puts the ums in in writing that he doesn't put in in speaking.

42

Beauty is not yet part of his self-image, so that's even more charming.

43

It's interesting when one of us is wearing more clothes than the other.

44

Being smart is only a job for them; they don't take it home.

45

There are people who, by acting nice and sharing their gifts, inspire rage in others and are the victims of cruel pranks, unjust treatment.

46

"See you around." "Around," she repeats as though hearing it for the first time. And what an ugly concept roundness is.

47

What was happening between these two people was more interesting than what was happening at the level of the game, between the teams.

48

He backs away from the curb to show that he is not waiting for a bus.

49

Pornography is more interesting when viewed upsidedown.

50

She agreed that her throw had not gone anywhere near the target.

51

Nothing angers them more than the suggestion that the recipients of their degrees were undeserving.

52

He grew up and immediately lost all his hair.

53

The joke is that where they economize is always security.

54

Not being at home

=

not knowing where there's privacy

A guest has no privacy.

55

It's easier for us to invent something new than to make an effort to understand the art that already exists.

56

I can't believe you're friends with that guy.
—Well you're friends with him.
Yeah I just can't believe you are.

57

I compulsively reminded them that it was still possible for me to fail.
They should not have to be reminded.

58

Aesthetic principles: nonrecurrent events and abrupt endings.

59

What are they doing with their time?
Mostly they worry . . .

60

People invent things to say.
This is the whole problem.
It's their job to say something, so they can't not say something, so they invent false issues.

61

“The least autobiographical writer.”
Everything I write is something I’ve thought.

62

Our wonderful Arabic numerals.

63

Flying into Minneapolis?
It’s like a dream.
It’s like the hippogriff.
It’s like “Dumbo.”

64

Career advancement is apparently not a sufficient motivation.

65

Cognitive portrait.
An amazing memory for things he hasn’t seen.
The least negatively capable person you ever met.

66

I wish I’d gotten bad grades.

67

A warrior is someone who keeps accidentally killing people.

68

Almost painful to keep from following a glance, a pointing finger, a command to look ("Look!").

69

A polite phrase uttered at an impolite volume.
A command: "Take your time!"

70

Why do people who don't know me want to take my picture?
This is too intimate to be shared with a stranger.

71

Slowing a door (so as not to let it slam shut) causes it to creak.
Preparation for bed refreshes you, puts off sleep.

72

"I couldn't sleep, but I thought I might be able to levitate."

73

So much language comes out of that guy.

74

"You're very sexy when you're disgusted."

75

Their clothes seem to show what they think their bodies are.

76

Touching the image, you expose yourself to contamination.

77

As though you could get there faster by pacing back and forth.

78

You've got to stop meeting everything with laughter.

79

Nodding and bowing to the telephone.

80

He would not knowingly wear any patterned fabric.

81

Only a successful American office worker can be truly innocent.

82

What about him? What percent is art, what percent is sheer pigheadedness.

83

Can someone just "pretend" to be nice?
Isn't being nice strictly on the level of appearance?

84

Will you let me say it as a joke?

85

Obviously these questions are formulas.

86

What answer would "you" give to such aggressive questions?

87

The closeness of the recently broken up.

88

He turned to look at her when she had completely finished speaking.

89

Some rooms, when you turn out the light, go red; others go green.

90

His description is so compelling that she decides to apply it to herself: "I'm like that too."

91

He wanted to believe that he was not choosing.

92

He is trying to annoy her, but she will not allow herself to be annoyed.

Finally, as an indulgence to him, she pretends.

93

People have almost no imagination; without other people they would surely die of boredom.

Fortunately not everyone has the same little imagination.

94

He always takes women to the same place, because he has no imagination.

95

I was telling him my problem.

I was not asking for his advice.

96

well honestly I feel
more comfortable in things that conceal

97

They all seem to prefer that one for their friend, never for themselves.

98

She thought I was making it up.
It was perverse for her to accept the invitation if she thought that—which means she thought I didn't want her here.
In any case, I wasn't making it up; it was quite true.
This should be rewritten.

99

No one says: "I like being in groups."
"I'm a follower."

100

Let's lose contact.

101

It's hard to tell, from what they're saying, if one of them is being reasonable.

102

And wasn't this also reflected in the style, the way each sentence seemed to occur three times or more.

103

Notice that his imagined "perfect day" does not include any imaginary encounters with other people.
No room for other people in his imagination.

104

They gave their children a traditional religious upbringing without telling them.

105

He pretends not to be a nice person.
Another one pretends to be nice.

106

Like an easy mark. Also like it's not worth the risk.
Like he's wearing a sign: "FUCK WITH ME."

107

He tells time by overhearing others ask for the time, or by reading their watches.

108

They don't quite match their sad or angry photographs.

109

The surface was not reflective enough to catch his imperfections.

110

He enjoys the weight swinging and twisting at the end of his arm.

111

Some parts of the body are never in fashion.

112

The finishing touch can hurt.

113

Seeing them with another person, they sometimes become more interesting. What you're not giving them becomes apparent.

114

The puffs of air escaping from his backpack.

115

"Thanks. I like to have a basin when I'm throwing up."

116

the filthiest thing I've ever touched
is the handle of your toothbrush

117

Punishment of the body is one of the needs of the soul.

118

If people had been nicer to her—really, if they had just left her alone—she might still be here.

119

I can hear you smiling.
The crack of his smile.

120

Everything else in the room was more interesting than the film.

121

Can't you blur me a little more?

122

Headline: BE SPECIFIC.
Or: BE MORE SPECIFIC.

123

He asked *very* nicely.

124

He'll even tell you what to think.

125

Same values, different suits.
Like with playing cards.

126

Yes we are relevant, yes we are exciting, just give us the money.

127

Yelling at her, but quietly, so awful to watch.

128

He waits until he's standing in front of the microphone, then blows his nose.

129

His tiredness made a sound that woke him.

130

He felt, at last, that he would be able to sleep at the poetry reading.

131

Warning: THIS PROGRAM HAS NO CONTENT.

132

Your two bad aspects are in conflict.

133

Nice job.

—My job is being nice.

134

Their parents murder them. And if they don't get murdered, they get married, and their spouses murder them in fits of jealousy. And their lovers murder their spouses.

135

Conversation is my form of suffering.

136

After ten minutes, conversation hits a wall.
Because you do not share anything with them, and the necessity of explaining everything, including the most elementary ideas, is unappetizing, and simulating agreement is impossible.

137

"Now you have to do something nice for someone else."
"I'd rather just pay cash."

138

I was pretty sure that I had behaved honorably.

139

He expresses love by spending money.

140

How often one is required to explain oneself.
Amazing that it should ever come as a surprise.
You don't have a prepared explanation?

141

dozing all afternoon
in the posture of the hanged man

142

Every time I looked at you you were reading, i.e., elsewhere.

143

The most important tool is ear plugs.

Masculinity is a rare thing

[November 2002-May 2003]

1

Contorted in a full-body scowl.

2

the sweep of your pants
fills me with dread

3

The choice between having a problem and introducing a fixer into the household—I will always choose the problem rather than the fixer.

4

When you start quitting, that sometimes becomes a substitute for the drug. You look for more things to quit—restricted diet, missing appointments, etc.

5

Mention of war still has the power to shut me up.

6

It's okay to like him because he has no influence.

7

Without waiting for his thoughts to settle, he started talking.

8

He almost leaps out of his chair, extends his arms as if to stop himself, or to stop someone across the room, from rising.

9

It becomes serious without anyone's taking it seriously.

10

I'll just leave you with your enthusiasm for that subject.

11

Is correct English more easily taught than affectionate response?

12

Worth the price of not joining.

13

I keep thinking I haven't read it, because it's so short.

14

Clearly someone was going to have to perform that task, as it had been performed in the past by someone.

15

An allergic reaction to people in cat costumes.

16

No one's ever talked to me that way except for a cop.

17

This means something, but one might almost wish that it did not.

18

He can't face hearing the verdict.
He would rather die than have someone make a decision.

19

You assume that people who resemble one another and agree with one another probably are friends.

20

Pretty soon you have five statues, all talking.

21

The same devices that the critics said he was too much of an artist to use, the critics now say that we who use them are excessively artistic—not, however, the same critics.

22

Analysis revealed two kinds of art.

23

It can't do more than kill you a little faster.

24

I've been smiling all day in anticipation of this, but I should have been afraid.

25

They woke up one morning in 1985 and discovered that everyone agreed with them.
They were dismayed by universal agreement.
"You understand my argument, so you think you agree with me."
"You think you agree with me, but you don't even understand my argument."
They had no one left to argue with but each other.

26

What is the tilt of Sharon's head?

27

The uncomplaining tenants.
Listen to the people upstairs make the discovery that there's no water.

28

At the first sign of trouble he starts to hoard water.

29

The kind of boyfriend who keeps calling, after he's broken up with you, to see how you're doing.

30

Shitty weather outside and in.

31

In the dream, I couldn't even remember your name.

32

Some communities hate awkwardness; others are in love with it.

33

Gratuitously being herself, just as gratuitously as he was himself.

34

The awkwardness that inevitably follows the one night stand—without, in this case, its having actually occurred.

35

It's like losing your native language.
Because there's no one else to speak it.

36

Not seeing him or hearing from him makes it harder to forget him, perhaps.

37

He looks at the ceiling. "Shut up, rain, you old fool, etc."

38

She talks almost as fast as she thinks; I talk a little faster than I think.

39

The cards are keeping you from your work.
But you're playing cards only because of the work.

40

There's nothing I can do that isn't work.

41

The person has to be asleep for the machine to work properly.

42

They have so much emotion for other people, when they see each other, they have to laugh.

43

Are we supposed to agree, or just prevented from disagreeing?

44

She senses that he is about to ask if he can borrow the car.

45

Not real enough to be memorized.

46

Too complex to be organic.

47

It's called figurative language. I used to worry about that; now I don't.

48

Or is your book a pump for dispensing poison.

49

In a bookstore, without money.
—I go to the bookstore to read.
In a video store, without money. To watch the movie on the monitor, to look at the boxes.

50

He does not speak of it because he could not put it in the past tense.

51

I've given you many receipts, but I hope none that will embarrass you.

52

Eventually one learns to resent those who do favors for one.

53

A rather elaborate sentence, for a newspaper.

54

You've protected yourself enough that you don't need compliments.
You don't know what to do with them.

55

His reply would have been astonishing.
Because he did not speak, only he was astonished.
His reply was astonishment.

56

She has to share it with the one person who doesn't notice.

57

Sometimes they prefer what they actually hear to what they wanted to hear.

58

For him, it's easier to lie in front of people who know he's lying. The lie gives him a coherence he is not usually able to find through talk.

59

Try not to give him something that he might spill.

60

Not an expressive face.
But it doesn't hide effectively.

61

Information is stored in the pen, not in the paper.

62

I try to incorporate some language from business into my conversation because I am so unbusinesslike.

63

For a better vantage point from which to watch you nibble on those orange sections.

64

Her mouth continued to open and close when there were no more orange sections, and she put in a piece of gum.

65

She "hated the telephone." Meaning that she had to share it with one person and resented anyone else's share in it.

66

The embarrassment of telling someone else's lie.

67

I used to think that politics was pretty much the same anywhere.

68

She loves to pick up men. She will never stop doing that, even when she stops sleeping with them.

69

That expression which he so often has in photographs—of trying not to be too much of a pill.

70

He stumbles over the beautiful word.

71

They have made up their minds individually but not collectively.

72

He's performing. He's performing badly.
He's performing obviously but not convincingly.
And it's not even recognizable as the performance we paid to see.

73

I answer to basically any pronunciation of my name, as well as the names Alex, Adam, Arthur, and Eric.

74

Warm pages and cold pages.
"I'll heat them up for you"—meaning, I'll copy them.

75

Certain emotions make you less distinct as a person.

76

Never quite getting over his original discomfort around phones.

77

If you had anything to ask you should have asked me; if you had anything to tell you should have told me.

78

"When did you learn to talk?"
I still do not think of myself as able to talk.
One of those personal myths to which I revert.

79

Something lacking in his saliva—it did not activate the glue on a stamp.

80

Not used to the clothes, the bag, or the food.

81

To think that what I had communicated to them was something that they could value, was my mistake.

82

A witness but saw nothing.

83

"inviting a friend to suffer"

84

Everyone had learned to imitate his affected manner, either to make him appear ridiculous or because they secretly wished to adopt similar mannerisms.

85

Or else what happens is something more like pity: it turns out to be "better than you expected," "better than you dared to hope."

86

With me he had the same relationship that he has with everyone. An example of no imagination.

87

Doing his best to ignore the persistent attempts to entertain him.

88

Struck (in the eye) by a histrionic gesture.

89

The most important part of them is not what they think but what they can't think. Because they have so little imagination.

90

Everything he says is followed by "I think."

91

The only available size is "large."

92

"You're playing a part that's too old for me."

93

I never joke about suicide.

94

I give that city too much power because I was unhappy there, and I give this city too much power for the opposite reason.

95

A sudden urge to let it fall into the trash can.

96

"I am not willing to perform. May I please be reseated."

97

Stolen information.
As the lights came up, his finger was in his nose.

98

Her face seen for the first time in the newspaper.

99

Spiritual and sexual doubt.

100

The flaw in the portrait is that it is not sufficiently human.
The flaw in the sitter is that he is not sufficiently human.

101

The mysterious appeal of humility.

102

The farthest distance at which I am identifiable is not a distance at which I am able to identify others.

103

Norms live in the mouth.

104

He blames her for something that's her job.

105

Nothing more embarrassing than lying badly.
And amusing.

106

"I don't believe it," in a voice whose credulous tone says the opposite.

107

The problem with his morality is that it's based on his relations with imaginary figures, not his actual relations.

108

You were doing such a good job reading books and watching movies in Baltimore, we brought you to Providence to read books and watch movies here.

109

I get annoyed at art that asks me to participate, which is just to say that I don't like being told how to participate.

110

To think that what I had unmummified was something of benign value, was my mistake.

111

Sometimes you find yourself lying. You make up trivial differences. You give an incorrect date, for example. Or are vague where you could be definitive.

112

The machine registering her voice is more interesting than her face registering her voice.

113

I'm taking his side against her because I'm on her side.

114

Deftly avoiding imaginary obstacles.

115

You can't offend more than one person at a time.

116

Censored or improved.
They may prefer the censored version.

117

I get paid to be polite.
And to wear the hat.

118

My heart is not red.

119

I used to take a long walk at 12 or 1 in the morning, because the air was cooler then.
The best time of day was probably a few hours later, while I slept.

120

He starts talking about an earlier discomfort because you're making him uncomfortable.
That's his only way of telling you.

121

Obviously you're suppressing it because you want it to be discovered.

He wants it to be seen; they don't want to see it.

Because no one wants to see what's on the surface.

Because the surface is inherently uninteresting.

Only Isaac Babel wants to see what's in front of him.

122

A shoe is not really very interesting.

123

Everything depends on where you put the divisions.

124

He had devoured the margins of his textbooks.

Semper Kunin semper pudor

[May-August 2003]

1

This class was "full of unmind."

2

You reacted too violently: "I never said that!"
And pleased: "Where did you hear it?"

3

Unable to distinguish a rumor he had circulated.

4

He lifts the foil from the yogurt container.

5

He won't allow himself to hurt her, so he will have to be satisfied with hurting her beautiful old friend.

6

Most people, when giving an excuse, are emphatically declining (both declining and giving a reason); however, this one turns out to be persuadable.

7

Surprisingly persuadable, for one so confident in her views.

8

His voice so low you know he's lying.

9

Will my voice continue to do the same thing?

10

After a lifetime of competing for objects that no one wants, against people who are only too happy to get out of her way, at last her competitive instinct rouses her to compete against those who are also competing.

11

Those who knew him recognized that pause.

12

Those who have jobs envy those who don't.

13

"Small talk." Right. My talk is very small.

14

A monitor of other people's looks: they must remain identifiable. They don't want you to keep your hair at that length because they think it's flattering; they want to be able to recognize you from a certain distance.

15

People tend to use the vocabulary you give them, because they have no imagination.

16

"You must be Aaron."

Not flattered. I did not appear as I wanted to be remembered.

17

He looks angry: because this is not how he wants to be remembered.

18

Sleeping without a list.

19

They did not want to hire someone creative in any sense of the word.

20

It seems easy because they don't know how to show difficulty. "You make it seem effortless" is not a compliment.

21

A poor ambassador for poetry. Because she makes it look easy.

22

"You make it look so difficult." Good.

23

Laconic "good."
Spiteful "good."

24

Unsure of my power, when so much has been given, so much assumed.

25

Distrust of rhetoric. "I feel this only because of something you deliberately said."
Fear of showing emotion. Suspicion of emotion that's shown.
"Your apparent emotion is only rhetoric."
"My emotion is an involuntary response to your rhetoric."

26

"How do you shave in there?" (*Charade*)
What's the answer?

27

The profession pretends to value both originality and conformity, both of which it calls professional.

28

Why do I have to carry my lunch so that everyone sees it.

29

You should know that I'm involved with someone—mentally.

30

What is frightening about symmetry.

31

Just blaming you.
No love, just blame.
Just blurring you.

32

The word "sincere" still ringing in his mouth.

33

Why books? Why didn't I study something lighter?
—Even a weightless thing, someone would be writing thick, heavy books about it.

34

She was excessively hungry, and closed her mouth around the spoon a little too soon. Instead of her mouth staying in place while the end of the spoon entered, her mouth seemed to leap out, snapping at the spoon so that her teeth clanked against it and wrenched it momentarily out of her fingers.

35

Boston, you always turned on the faucet for me.

36

The book mumbled.

37

then perhaps it is
my book after all

38

It goes in both directions but exerts different pressures depending on what it's facing.

39

I have a good memory for that kind of thing, because I have little else to remember.

40

The repeated "good."
I repeat: "good."

41

I can make it sound better than that.

42

"Right," he said unhappily.
With private unhappiness.

43

Not able to demonstrate the requisite happiness.

44

I rarely pause for emphasis—awaiting, making space for, a response.
I skip spaces for emphasis, voiding response.

45

You showed too much delight in being handled by a particular person.

46

And something like this is, after all, done on computers.

47

I need to look at my shoes for a second.

48

He has said it so many times it's not really a joke.
After many repetitions it's hardly a joke.

49

No solace in his own education.

50

He's suspicious of the idiom that his voice readily produces.

51

Sleeping on the bus.
With his chin resting on the open scrapbook.
A picture of his family history shielding his chest.

52

A formerly ironic relationship.

53

He adjusted the height of his pants, shaking a bit to keep the tail of his shirt in.

54

Of course he's going to keep talking while he stands at the urinal.

55

Almost nothing is more interesting than a crying baby.

56

Fallen partly asleep.

Measured by the tilt of his head.

57

Sing that which is concrete.

She calls it that because that's the material she's going to strike.

58

A smile flowed over his face.

A smile bloomed at the bottom of his face.

59

They take it as a confirmation of what they always believed.

They use it as a pretext for doing what they secretly wanted to do.

60

Even I have been tempted by an unchained bicycle.

61

At first politics merely feels good.

62

"I don't want to see any movie in which this, this, or this happens to a woman."

63

I was meant to be an energetic accomplished person.
In my childhood I was always extremely hungry.

64

One reason why people read novels and watch movies is that they like to see women being tortured.
—Do they like to see it on every page, in every frame?

65

Books, cups, plates, newspapers—cut into the table.

66

Or do you have to be invited in like a vampire.

67

Brian has to tie his shoe; it might take a while.

68

Distinction between the color of an object and the color it makes.
"Pencil yellow" names a color.
Pencils are yellow, but they do not make yellow.

69

He goes back so that he can walk out.
This time he knows exactly when to leave.

70

It's really good, but it's worth more than anyone can afford to pay for it.

71

How can they be geniuses on that amount of food?

72

It took him at least a week to unlock the mysteries of the electric kettle.

—Partly a superstition prohibiting the combination of water and electricity; partly a backwardness in dealing with machines.

73

She finds that "if she pays attention" her food usually turns out all right.

74

Flirtation is by nature incomplete.

75

If you can't remember your name, you might choose "Aaron"—it's likely to be the first one you encounter on an alphabetical list.

76

"Do you have a library card?"
What if we used books rather than cars to identify people.

77

This child needs to be given nourishing food because of all that he might accomplish.

78

She wasn't mature enough to handle the responsibility of two boyfriends.

79

A certain kind of person, if you buy a new pair of shoes, will notice immediately, even if you're not wearing the shoes.

80

I could never be seriously involved with you, because we're not awake at the same time of day.

81

Will you please take this knife out of my forehead.

82

The smartest thing we did was to schedule our rendezvous to coincide with the department meeting; thus, the meeting became much more interesting.

83

They cared about it enough to lie about it.

84

Tendency to look down when shaking hands.

85

The fan looks around vibrating.

86

When her tape starts playing, she can't pause or stop it.
Usually she has to let it play twice.

87

The engineer of nasty solutions.
"Engineering nasty solutions since 1978"
Someday I'll puzzle over that.

88

The entire audience has the same response.
Everyone has to try it.
You can't resist looking at your own hand.

89

No applause. Everyone is too busy staring at their hands.

90

When did you learn consciousness of being watched.

91

I remember shaving before we met.

92

For a moment he had been thinking of himself as a fictional character.
Trying to recall his "traits."

93

I could see his tortured soul.

94

He would rather wash his own dish because then he would be in the kitchen, away from these awful people.

95

Dangerous when someone so eloquent is angry.

96

Feminist bookstore replaced by poor Italian restaurant.

97

Unbuttoning the lowest button on his vest is to admit defeat.

98

"She says she's meeting friends but she's alone."

99

Agreement. We don't lose each other in places where we expect others to get lost.

100

"I would like to"

=

"in another possible world 'I would like to'"

101

Walking on what I consider the shady side of the street, baffled by sunlight, because it's a few hours earlier than my usual walk.

102

Whatever I do will partly define what is acceptable.

103

Leave the price tag on.

"It's now considered socially acceptable, and even interesting, to wear the garment with the price tag attached."

104

He answered the phone, although the chances of its being for him were certainly very slight.

105

In my apartment, including the bathroom, there are no mirrors. In the kitchen, I am trying to find my reflection in a pan lid, the blade of a knife, etc., in which I am partly discernible but as a shadow without much detail.

106

One goes to work either to enjoy the company of others ("company") or to be alone.

107

In so many ways one pays others for the privilege of working for them.

108

Hornets building a nest behind a NO PARKING sign.

109

I do my own paperwork.

Protected from machines, not from paper.

110

Shrugging grotesquely in an effort to maintain his sense of humor.

111

Talking in sleep, when it can't be helped, may be preferable to talking while awake, when it can.

112

Whether you eat it (through the mouth) or internalize it some other way.

113

An emotion suggested by war monuments.

The book of which I alone was ashamed

[September 2003-April 2004]

1

When I say that something is not interesting I usually mean that its design is completely predictable and it is not well made.

2

Barely alive, hardly autonomous, and not even cute.

3

Tie a knot in a plastic bag and it feels like a bag of dog shit.

4

He is intelligent, and highly educated, and that's all his writing says: "I am intelligent."

5

Modernism is what we got instead of communism.

6

Both sides of the bread are buttered.

7

How much of life is spent looking away from what one feels one should not have seen.

8

The wrong kind of love—i.e., a god's.

9

You interrupted me, made me cross the floor, just to say hello, not for any other conversation.

10

All the papers that pass through his hands try to look important; sometimes it's difficult to remember which ones he wants to pay attention to.

11

"Desert Island Discs" is really a way of noticing that you have too many discs.

12

If you were awake it would be easy enough to make a decision. But in the dream it seems hard to remember that you can't have everyone.

13

He kicked a rock, and it screamed. "The rock cried out."

14

Not the kind of room where everything has its place.

15

Boo! Oh sorry, didn't mean to scare you.
—Then you shouldn't say boo.

16

The good guy.
Or, really, the "good enough" guy.
Or, therefore, the "radically evil" guy.

17

An accurate, if not flattering, representation.

18

Dream: reading, contrary to my promise, "I Despise Your Life" by Patricia Highsmith.

19

Almost for politeness, he stayed in bed very late. So that she could have the house to herself for some time? So that she would not think she had disturbed his rest?

20

He would be unlikely to recognize that it came from a particular person; however, he might be able to recognize it as an idea he dislikes.

21

Within the body some adjustment was audibly taking place.

22

It assumes a definite shape if you forget to wash it.

23

He looked at me with suspicion, as though I was trying to trick him into admitting a shameful practice.

24

Some of us have ideas; some only have words.

25

"I'll give it some thought." Tugging, tugging, on the skin around his eyes, to flatten his face.

26

He looks at me. And I look at myself: this time, maybe I am about to say something?

27

"There's a fetish in the kitchen"—i.e., the microwave.

28

Food alone?
Sex alone?
Food and sex.
Civilization.

29

I feel great!
—Maybe it's because you had lunch?

30

The speaker apologizes for the absence of the introducer.

31

Loved it enough to write about it; hated it enough to leave.

32

If you want to understand shame, just look down.

33

Those who should know best are most likely to forget.

34

Although I don't have a body, I can produce the impression of one through layering and gluttony.

35

If it has enough intelligence to dissimulate in order to preserve its comforts, then it especially deserves my respect and care.

36

Because she always has something to say.
And when she says it she always goes farther than the last person.

37

One can never be sure until afterwards whether one should have gotten out of bed or not.

38

A woman trying to write on a man's arm.
"Stop it."
"You can wash it right off."
"Let me just finish this one finger."
"Quit moving."

39

People almost always work with the vocabulary you give them, because they have no imagination.

40

If I stop and think, I might never start talking again.

41

Just the fact that someone has tried to follow your instructions is deeply satisfying.

42

Rejecting women was his life's work and he wanted to spend a lot of time on it.

43

She narrates his failure to reply.

44

"The surface will not stop making a nice conclusion"
(dream sentence)

45

No one is only one color.

46

Their production was so inept that it put him into analysis.

47

Most comfortable with his left hand planted on the topmost part of his head.

The very top of his head. Indicating his highest elevation. A reminder of his dimensions.

48

Come over to my house, maybe I'll give you a piece of cake.

49

What is the meaning of that shake of the head, what is he denying.

50

A fit of coughing drove her from the room.

51

We get angry at others who do their work especially well.

52

Motto: "slow down quickly."

53

After talking for about five minutes, he reached the edge of his thinking, and, as usual, he was not able to slow down quickly enough to avoid going over the edge.

54

In the front row, scowling.

55

They always tell you when they know they have exceeded the recognized limit.
They know exactly how far to go, and they go farther, and they tell you that they have done it.
They know exactly what they are doing.

56

He's quick. And, therefore, quick to take offense, quick to retaliate.

57

You depend too much on art and rest.

58

He shows what he's thinking and it doesn't matter.
His innermost thoughts are made manifest and still no one notices.

59

Some people invent their practice, but most do not have that much imagination.

60

Leave the knife in the sofa.

61

I was wrong about being in pain.

62

With regard to the arrangement of one's house—one is blind. Insofar as one lives anywhere one is blind.

63

She understood. And she knew that it would be more interesting if she understood it differently than he intended.

64

You want to agree with what you are reading.

65

The most sensitive people see things that are not there.

66

Are you sensitive?
—I like to avoid being yelled at if that's what you mean.

67

Cynicism is generally pleased by independent confirmation.

68

"I want to dress him."

"I want to put my hand on her shoulder."

"I want to be a few inches shorter than her."

69

You understand me better than I understand you.

70

"I am a rogue, and all the world knows it. What the world doesn't know is that you also are a rogue. But I know it; and I'm the only one in the whole sweet world who does. And I could let the rest of the world in on the secret; and I could make a pretty convincing case—little as my word is worth, rogue though I may be."

71

A cigarette to indicate the mouth.

Or instead of a mouth.

A cigarette projecting from a face.

72

You looked like a prisoner when we first met.

73

He took two or three glasses.
He took two glasses, then a third.

74

You never know how far people will go in their effort to prevent you from getting real information.

75

She cut off their developing argument and drew their irritation to herself.

76

She doesn't want to be told that she looks worried.

77

By his own reckoning he had made exceptions for—practically everyone.

78

He sits down to prove he's tired.

79

Both gratifying and insulting.
Take your pick, and respond in kind.

80

I'm asking you to do something extremely difficult that has almost no value.

81

You can't expect to be rewarded for invisible qualities.

82

"We belong to the family of puppets."

83

"I thought that I was talking to you, but you are a puppet; I was talking to another person who invisibly controls you."

84

Unable to recall the sensation of the tip of the pen striking the paper.

85

I got him to agree to something before he saw what the conversation was about.

86

"She could be persuaded" to commit adultery.

87

When the Norton Anthology calls to tell me that they want to make me irrelevant by reproducing some of my writing, I will gladly come to terms and celebrate my obsolescence by giving a series of boring lectures, but I do not want to be a "younger American poet"!

88

I do not feel any obligation to be what the newspaper tells me I am.

89

Was anyone ever punished for misogyny?

90

Completely satisfied by minimal evidence of humanity and intellect, e.g., a voice saying hello and your name.

91

Could he be using that tone of voice to address me? He is obviously addressing an infant.

92

As he talked, he seemed to hold me between his fingers and crumple me up.

That is what he was doing with his hand on the way home.

93

To compromise her power of action.
This is the purpose of asking advice.

94

When you want advice, you want a person's advice. What the person will say is usually not a surprise. Choosing an advisor, you also choose the advice you will be given.

95

But you do not always intend to follow the advice that you choose to hear. Sometimes you want to hear advice that you do not intend to follow; hearing it supports the other course of action.

96

Those who do not like making decisions also do not like asking for or taking advice—because these are also decisions.

97

Sunglasses?
—I prefer to wear a blindfold. Or an eyepatch.

98

Discovery that there is nothing of interest in the backpack.
Disgust.
—Steal it anyway.

99

A surprisingly foul mouth when left to himself.

100

You can't blame them for believing what you tell them.
You shouldn't.

101

Showing that you have information usually shows how you got it.

102

Just having the thought shows that you are more than sufficiently prepared to do it.

103

I carry it to prove that it no longer has any explanatory power.

104

In the past ten years she has basically eliminated surprise.

105

Take your evidence with you.

106

He decided to have a renaissance.
And he decided to pay for it.

107

A poetic idea: burning up calories in the body.

108

He could always be counted on to produce a pen.
Contents of his pockets: pen, keys, wallet / notebook, watch.
The notebook and pen would be produced from opposite sides.
A two-handed operation—writing and supporting the notebook.
Holding. Being held. "Composure."

109

Ability without achievement.
Achievement without accomplishment.
Accomplishment without promotion.

110

Work without job.
Job without career.
Career without vocation.

111

And no money.

112

At least you can be interesting and pleasant.
You never were indispensable.

113

We want things whose value is illusory which nonetheless we don't deserve.

114

Should I ask? Or should I assume that I will eventually be able to derive an answer without having to embarrass or commit myself by asking a direct question?

115

People ask if they have satisfactorily answered my question. —And, indeed, it rarely happens. Sometimes they apologize for not really answering.

116

If our laws were enforced, our lives would be unbelievably awful.

117

"Ah," meaning I understand, or that I don't.

118

I often ask questions for which even the form of the answer is not obvious.

119

I have often said, with an undefinable feeling, "I love being what I am."

120

I assume that I will be the same person, with the same energies and abilities, for the rest of my life.

121

"Yours" is really superior as a signatory; it expresses affection, and I like affectionate formalities.

"Best," abbreviation of "best wishes," is more distant and vaguely presumptuous—as though the best were mine to give—but it has become deeply ingrained in me through repeated use.

I like that we frame communications with love, respect, fidelity, sincerity.

122

To what extent have you been deformed by the faulty end of your pen? And the necessity of scratching three times to make one mark?

123

Graphological portrait.

Looks more like a person than a letter.

A "written character."

124

If I do this to myself, imagine what I'm going to do to you!

125
When aroused, he would inhale forcefully through his nose, which sometimes made him sneeze.

126
He was forced to cancel the lecture because of a suspicious growth on the underside of his tongue.

127
Their compromises do not compromise them.
All make compromises for their ambition.
It is not the compromises that are used against them but the ambition. They will gladly admit the compromises (which were always intended for public view) but never the ambition.

128
I asked him a second time just to see him stammer and act confused.

129
Where in your house do you feel most comfortable?

130
I never hear names I only hear specialties.

131
All your girlfriends have the same handwriting.
What your handwriting would look like if it got cleaned up.

132

She ends with happiness, not with certainty.
A certain ending.

133

It's practically the only moment in his collected works in which the first person is active and the second person is passive; therefore I revised it to make it consistent with the whole.

134

They give each other something to think about. They really don't make each other happy, do they?

135

I remember laughing very hard at something, but it was so silly I couldn't repeat it.

136

oh lovely lemon tree
that grows over my first boyfriend's head

137

People manage to pay for my coffee and food only because I'm not the first one inside the store.
Very true.

138

I feel like that.

A tattered edge.

You were not torn out along the perforation.

How you were torn out carelessly.

139

"I used shoe polish on my hair."

"I can tell."

Unable to stop touching the shining top of her head.

140

When have I ever left a book lying open or a newspaper unfolded?

141

How can he have so much work when he has no job?

142

It's actually quite interesting to watch someone fail to execute a gesture.

143

Amused; laughs; ashamed (his laugh too masculine); he smirks into his hand.

144

A crack might have been heard from his pocket as the end of the pen cap he had been fiddling with broke off.
An obsessive practice that he wasn't even aware of.

145

He is not sensitive enough to notice that his friend is not the same person.

146

Each question seemed to strike her and she struck her own chest for emphasis.

Sex and serious

[May-December 2004]

1

Walking and crawling.

2

He slept well, but it was not good for him.

3

What you read determines not what you think, but what you imagine others are thinking.

4

On the cover of my mother's copy of *The Complete Novels of Jane Austen*: the back of a woman's head, enclosed in a bonnet, giving the impression of an enormous beetle.

5

Did I look at you today?
Do I care about you today?

6

To make it official.
To seem official.

7

I'm laughing at it because I don't understand it.
They're scared of it because they don't understand it.
Their attitude is more realistic.

8

We have all made drawings.
We have all composed music, and perform it.

9

Rolling her eyes at her own diction.

10

Those who were offended apologize.

11

Please be courteous. Please be curt.

12

Or would you rather listen to them talk about music.

13

The pathetic effort of public signage to make itself universally legible.

14

“Modernism is good enough for us.”

15

Ibsen carried a mirror in the brim of his hat for the purpose of staring at himself. Just staring.

16

One would expect a psychology so totally outside the field of human possibility to be at least interesting.

17

Your students don't look like you.
—Failed teacher?

18

I found myself wanting him to like and respect me, although I did not like or respect him particularly.

19

You rely too much on your personal charm. Which in your case is especially dangerous because charm is what your enemies will attack you for.

20

What you are saying provokes them to enter the conversation while you are still saying it.

21

He involuntarily looked at the shelf as he said this—as though he was putting something on it.

22

Merely annoying (not in a sexual way).

23
He folds up charmingly
in his chair
in your pocket

24
Were they talking or were they nodding silently.

25
Proud of her boyfriend.
His accomplishments.
With an almost maternal pride.

26
Colors are still mostly invisible.
Sounds are mostly inaudible.

27
Pulling his face back to stay awake.

28
The dangerous place where you are required to act or speak and are not motivated to do or say anything—this is where you would follow any instruction unquestioningly.

29
One must say something; one must act; one follows instructions—there is that danger.

30

Leather and weather do not rhyme.

31

An unpleasant pressure caused by what he was going to say when I went out of the room.

32

He is, to use a phrase unfairly reserved for women, a piece of work.
He is a made thing.

33

An unwelcoming smile.

34

Notice: MAPS ARE FOR CUSTOMER USE ONLY.

35

"I just gave the *worst* directions."

36

His left leg vibrated until I looked at it.

37

When the head contends against the foot, the head tends to lose.
This is an example of bad administration.

38

He is already imagining not being with you.

And he's making plans to see you again.

39

Awkwardness and mistakes are necessary for producing the conjunctive relation.

40

An engineer of delightful solutions who uses awkwardness and mistakes: the novelist.

41

Left to their own devices, the sensitive could not form a relation between themselves; their relation depends on awkwardness imposed by others who are less sensitive.

42

His body projects this message: "Do not touch me."

43

I can predict their behavior, but I do not understand them.

44

He tried unsuccessfully to hide what he was unsuccessfully reading.

45

"if you knew me better, you would not compare me to him"

46

They are in trouble and they are in power.
Get power over them by giving them what they want.

47

Does he realize that he talks at perhaps quarter-speed.

48

When the most important part of you is preserved as a keepsake, it is unlikely that you will share the experience.

49

He's that way because someone did that to him.

50

An intelligent look suddenly crossed his face.

51

He does everything possible to convince himself that he exists: whistling, talking to himself, etc.
—Or is he trying to put you in his head where a tune is playing, where that phrase originates.

52

Not because they respect your privacy but because no one is sufficiently interested to violate it.

53

You have not been entirely successful in your campaign to look like an adult this afternoon.

54

Revealing unconscious activities: peeling labels off bottles; flattening straw, forcing it through front teeth; wiping hands on thighs; pulling up grass blades.

55

Those who talk have more to be ashamed of.
We do not lie awake regretting our silences.
Not to have spoken is always a cause for satisfaction.

56

He hates when people whistle tunes, scent their clothing, etc.
Because they do it for their own enjoyment, but everyone else has to enjoy it too.
A treat for all, whether they want it or not.

57

You get to choose your own replacement.

58

People who live in cities have trouble making decisions.

59

"First poem you ever loved?"
"I'd like to suggest that you marry it."

60

They do their job, which is dying beautifully; he does his job, which is taking their names.

61

Because he demands love indiscriminately and returns love unwillingly.

62

It's too much work to close her mouth and continue chewing.

63

You feel more confidence in writing than in talk, because you've rarely been humiliated in writing, because in our civilization writing happens in private.

64

You imagine yourself an object of fascination to your neighbors.

65

When did you learn to talk?

—Quite recently, I think, only this afternoon.

66

When he next opened his mouth, he had forgotten how.

67

His hands were shaking noticeably as we shook hands.

68

She looks angrily at those who remain, because she is really talking to the one who left.

69

He can't help answering, even if it's only mouthing the words.

70

I put my brain to sleep, instead of the usual procedure, which is letting my brain put me to sleep.

71

He said it to himself.

He couldn't get anyone else to say it.

72

Your watch has a broken nose.

73

Another time, instead of locking him in, she left with his wallet—so he couldn't go anywhere.

74

"Oh! I just realized that my boyfriend is locked in."

75

She asked if I had gone gay, and I was too embarrassed to explain my belief that academics should be celibate.

76

I reminded myself not to think of you.

77

What do I really understand about shame?

78

Unacceptable treatment accepted.

79

How does one know the correct word if one has never used it before and never seen it used?

80

All the voices inside you are singing in unison to justify your actions.

81

Codependence is sometimes used to mean something valuable, like sympathy.

82

Still maligning his predecessor, several years into the job.

83

You know extremely well how it works, yet you persist in using it as an index of value.

84

While doing something else, without thinking about it, he starts cleaning.

85

Graphological portrait.
Try to look like you're working.
Seated in odd positions, or standing and pacing.
Ah, he's writing; this looks like work.
If only the notebook were in a larger format.
What can he be working on. Such tiny pages, etc.
Nothing that could be shown easily since no one could read his little writing.

86

One awake at night, the other awake in the morning; they meet in the middle.

87

The most formal signatories are often the most intimate (although intimacy is hardly what they communicate).

88

Without effort he speaks, and even makes a joke.

89

With the unconcern that everyone has for those who may be sleeping, along with the special contempt that early-risers have for those who sleep through the morning.

90

We had both turned in the direction of her house to illustrate the conversation.

91

A flash of jealousy when she thought there was a girlfriend.
"No, you can still fold me up and put me in your pocket."
"You can continue to amuse yourself with me."

92

Proprietary feelings for someone whose feelings we would be surprised to learn we share.
An example of "feelings are always mutual."

93

Temptation to negotiate from a position of strength rather than weakness.

—Wrong. Because talking to them is weakness. For this behavior, I will not reward them with my conversation.

94

He carefully mentions the coordinates which he knows will be unintelligible.

95

She hears the words and can't help fidgeting.
The words make her want to dance.

96

They never remember what they reject.
Sometimes what they include is also forgotten.

97

You couldn't decide whether to be intimidated by him or amused by yourself.

98

"Errors of feeling." Which could mean an error caused by a feeling, or a mistake about someone else's feeling, or a wrong kind of feeling (rage, fear, pettiness, etc.).

99

The point is not that characters who are round are closer to being people.

The point is that some people are flat; others are round.

The distinction between round and flat is real.

100

They want immediate gratification but don't take it when it's offered.

101

"Ah!"

"You say *that* right."

102

I want to say to you: "The world would like you better if you were less brilliant, less fluent, and more modest. But for you to be any of these things would be dishonest."

103

Only read within his immediate family, and they were deeply offended by it, as they said to one another, but not to him.

104

I don't think you dreamed it, because you haven't slept.

105

The ability to do something seems to furnish a reason for doing it, but it is not a good reason.

106

"That sounds interesting."
"No. What I said was *not interesting*."

107

saying it is like
eating an apple
to cleanse the palate

108

"Interesting," the most value-laden term I allow myself—meaning, "This rewards serious consideration."

109

It's easier to talk about space when there are divisions. "There are no paths, but there is boundlessness," but how would she know, she never went out of the house?

110

She offers boundlessness as compensation, which is close to offering loss itself as compensation.

111

Sometimes there is no greater surprise than using a word correctly.

112

A laugh (more of a snort) passed from one head to another seated next to it and to the one seated next to that, as each one realized that what she had said was clever.
A row of snorts.

113

She read the novel while brushing her teeth, morning and night, and after snacks, over a period of several years.

114

He would have preferred to keep his hands in his pockets but worried that it might be dangerous.

115

Something the poet said made her want to lick the side of her boyfriend's face.

116

One can learn a lot by paying attention.
What I mean is that you learn a lot by paying attention; I generally do not.

117

They are both on the phone; neither is talking.

118

The look on her face said: “I am pretending to read.”

119

Every person has an accent.
Every object has a noise.

120

Your hard walk has undone the knot in your shoelace.

121

“More than welcome” means less.

122

He looked at me curiously, as if hoping to discover a legitimate reason for being angry with me.

123

Perhaps that’s what she wants; that’s her misguided way of asking for it.
Too bad, because she’s just smashed the chances of your giving it.

124

A person would never make such poor decisions except when trying to imagine what others want. Or trying to influence what they want.

125

Misunderstandings occur with those whose behavior we think we can predict.
What we mean by betrayal.

126

The awareness that someone has just looked at you, and the difficulty of not acknowledging it.

127

She felt part of herself being looked at.

128

As I held the door, he could see my disappointment.
He wanted to touch it.
He touched my arm, my inner elbow.

129

Capable of nothing deeper than the love a cat would feel for the person who gives it food.

130

If I could just break down completely in front of them twice a week, then they might learn something.

131

Writing on someone's arm without permission.
A true intellectual.

132

Keys, wallet, comb, keys, flask.
(Right to left.)
Two of these items are foreign to me.
I barely remember their names.

133

It would be useful for him to be in a situation where he is not exceptional.

134

Wearing armor does not make you feel invulnerable.
You feel aware. You are aware of where you are vulnerable, for example.

135

They moan every time the phone rings.
It's the cue for their part in a song.

136
To make it official.
To seem afraid.

137
To make it official.
To seem unreasonable.

138
To make it unreasonable.

139
Monkeys love starched shirts and collars.
Monkeys want to wear starched shirts (and collars).
Monkeys love yellow starch.

140
Someone else, working with the same materials, and given the same opportunities, might have done a better job.

141
There are two possibilities.
Either she's really kind of dumb or she thinks it would be cool to be dumb so she pretends.
I prefer to think she's really dumb, because it's more honest.
A third ungenerous possibility is that she's really dumb but thinks she's smart but likes to pretend to be dumb—both dumb and dishonest.

142

It's not rational to want to kill the whole organism.
It's rational to want to defeat your enemies.

143

It's not her fault that the rest of the world doesn't think this clearly.

144

The older torments the younger by insulting her appearance; the younger torments the older by confusing her mind.

145

I make a weak attempt to hold the door open, which thankfully you do not see.

146

"Words and flesh."
That's true. That's what people are made of.
The same flesh, different words—that's how you can tell us apart.

147

I gave him plenty of chances to do something offensive.

148

I hope everything that happens to you happens for a reason.
(curse)

149

Signage: AARON TAKES ADVANTAGE OF THE POOR.

150

I invented this concept, but I was able to do so only because someone else had already invented it.

151

You enter a room already occupied by several intelligent or at least highly educated people. And they are curious about you. They want to spend the next hour learning about you. But perversely they have directed their curiosity toward your least significant aspect, your knowledge of the English Renaissance.
They want to learn about you through the Renaissance.

152

I hang up the phone correctly.
There is a right way to hang up a phone.

153

The worst possible
The harshest part
The part in your hair

154

He wore it once; one of the buttons came off.
An unmistakable sign of poor workmanship.

155

They are thrilled to contribute.
Or they participate mechanically.
Or they are offended if you ask for a contribution.

156

A good place to begin stamping out inappropriate demands for love.

The collected lies of AK

[January-October 2005]

1

He slept on the floor because he had made his bed and wanted to remain in control of one part of life.

2

I was not made in a lab.
I was made in a factory!

3

I was not made in a bed.
I was made like a bed!

4

I thought that I had forgotten to ask, but it turns out I had forgotten the answer.

5

Books can crash too of course.
Just like computers!

6

He had not given up on the ambitions of modernism.
"Their importance will make me important."

7

"Make me look artificial."
"I want to look like a doll."

8

"I am a forty-year-old fat fuck."

"Well I'm not any of *those things*."

9

He gives her plenty of room because he knows she's afraid of him.

10

I always believe your whoppers.

Because I do not know what to do with figurative language.

11

From whom may we reasonably demand love?

12

It was not a long-distance relationship; it was just a distance relationship.

13

Easily touched and easily appeased.

True, he is easily touched (offended), but it's so pointless, because he is easily appeased.

14

Do you think I'm disguising my smell too much.

15

He suddenly produced that phrase and died laughing.

16

One vibrates; the other muffles.

17

I could not hear it because of the people I was sitting next to.

18

"I have been with you all day and now this mild presence is enough to light you up."

19

Not all cartoons are fun.
Cartoons are not fun.
Fun is restricted by conditions.
There is no fun.

20

"for FUN"
(put all possible stress and violence on "fun," make it scary and painful, it hurts to say it)

21

I always say it after I hang up the phone; one time, I said it before.

22

Sympathetic and contagious magic is the same idea!
Inductive and deductive reasoning is the same idea!
Illocutionary and perlocutionary is the same idea!
Showing and telling is the same idea!

23

Everything I can't tell the difference between.

24

A place in the airport without TV.
Seemingly less crowded because there is no TV.
One of your coworkers, the TV.

25

The anthropologist's suggestion: you lack culture, you do not interact with your group, you need TV.

26

Aren't you lonely without TV?

27

I felt my brow unfurrow.
I heard it.

28

Stop worrying your expression.

29

Please, he said.
He said please.

30

He never recognizes you first (because he doesn't wear his glasses).
Unless you are merely inches away from him, unless you are a particularly striking-looking person, he can't make you out.
His nearsightedness is frequently mistaken for rudeness, idiocy, harshness, etc.
This explains why all his friends have exaggerated features.

31

He is trying hard to make silence appear to be an ethical position.

32

He laughs because he realizes he has just said something rude.
He laughs to cover the insult.

33

Maybe unconsciously he's trying to sabotage you?
—Give him a little credit! He is aware that he is trying to sabotage me.

34

Now you can cross it off your list.
Assuming you can find the list.

35

I have destroyed your list!

36

She can't help inventing plausible stories.

37

You've heard me tell my version of the story; now I want to hear your version.

38

No, that's just what you wanted to hear; that's not what I said.

39

The gift of being sometimes alone.
The gift of being able to identify what you are feeling.

40

She has the unusual gift of knowing what she's feeling right now.
But she can hardly believe in what she has felt or will feel.

41

We assume that our procedures are transparent.

42

He breaks the rule twice.
Perhaps it isn't a rule.

43

Have you learned anything yet?
—Only the banal moral lesson of the age in which we live: when to silence your phone.

44

What used to keep you awake now disturbs or entertains you while you sleep.

45

He felt his expression change.
He felt it changing.

46

He suddenly looked up and said yes.

47

enjoying a cigarette
destroying a cigarette
worrying a cigarette

48

We kissed and it was like *Invasion of the Body Snatchers*. It was like kissing a pod.

49

Her most resilient quality is playfulness.
Her other spirits may be depressed, but her spirit of play never quits.
It's the part of her that can't die.
(The rest could die; that part will live on.)

50

I just got a new phone, and I wanted to try it out.
—Well it works.

51

When she says she is confused she knows exactly what she wants but can't ask for it directly.

52

Solve the problem by not calling back.

53

She made them forgive her in advance in case she "fucked up," "went crazy," etc.
But when the time came, she did not act crazy; her sanity was terrifying.
Her sanity was terribly convincing.

54

There is no difference.

—Between shouting in the street, singing, whistling, mumbling to yourself, talking on the phone in public, and writing in your notebook, and wearing perfume.

55

Grimaces made while making music.

56

One part of the body pulls on another, because they are all connected.

57

What do mistakes and endings look like?

58

For a second I didn't care.
For a second, brushing hair out of my eyes, I felt happy.

59

His hand goes to what he is thinking.
His hand follows his thoughts.

60

Affectations become habits until we are rescued from our habits by a love.

61

I become worse at the things I'm already bad at.
Talking is the first thing that suffers.

62

I hate that I am protective of my little knowledge.

63

I have never seen any man allow himself an expression of so much pain in a public place.

64

He curled up on the floor like a dog.
And shut his eyes and nodded like a dream of chasing or digging.

65

"I'm being serious," he said, laughing.

66

An unlikely candidate for suicide, which requires decisiveness.

67

It's the first thing to go.
When he's distressed, his playfulness is the first thing to go.
In distress, he gives up on play.
It wipes off easily.
—It was a very thin layer.

68

You made me forgive you in advance for going crazy, but when the time came for you to go crazy you did not act crazy; you were terribly sane.
Yes, your sanity terrified me.
And I forgive you for that.

69

"Sorry this is difficult." She apologizes for the difficulty, although it is easy enough to offend, to apologize, and to forgive.

70

That is what he could not understand. And that is how he knew it was true.

71

A smile is a kind of bite.
Because it's a hole in the face.

72

I have a better idea: why don't you go into the kitchen, find the carving knife, and plunge it repeatedly into my abdomen, here, here, and here?

73

"They're jerking off, and it isn't even spontaneous, it's rehearsed!"

74

A wreck: i.e., a kind of vehicle.

75

You were the primary obstacle to her happiness, and the instrument.

She brought you here to make herself happy; then made herself happy by getting rid of you.

Happiness solicited. And accomplished.

Unhappy instrument!

76

He stood on the porch, examining his motives.

He looked down, examining his motives.

77

They did not return together.

78

When you are called on to do the great work of making a person happy, it is terrible to fail in that task.

79

The essential fact about him is that he's a pod.

Or is the essential fact whose pod he is.

80

When I open my mouth, I die of embarrassment (every time).

81

She justifies her actions by referring to the actions of those who mistreated her.

82

I got here sooner than I was comfortable with, in order to gratify you.
And I do not regret it.
I do not regret anything I did with the intention of making you happy.
And, besides, "there is no substitute for someone who actually wants to see you."
Unfortunately, when I arrived, I was too tightly wound.

83

How terrible it would be if he should fail!

84

If only it were that simple.
If all that was necessary to your happiness was the correct recitation of passages from classical poetry.

85

At 2 a.m. he started to entertain bad thoughts about you.

86

bless the garbage can
at the library

87

When I think of all the calculations I have made in the cause of general politeness!

88

The standard by which you act is how you've been treated.

89

A question or an accusation.
You didn't ask if I was enjoying the film. You asked how I was doing.
And I said that I was okay—which was a lie; I was miserable.
You did not ask if I was grateful and I did not answer gracefully or graciously.

90

"cold seas of feeling ice"
(dream sentence)

91

People who are stupid are likely to do stupid things.
Smart people can get stupid people to do stupid things.
This kind of manipulation is not taxing to anyone's intelligence.
Stubborn is another story.

92

I loved Judith's body.
And her voice. She had three voices actually: one was small, another was sarcastic, the third was declamatory.
And her sense of smell.
And her puns.

93

She was satisfied and embarrassed by what she said.

94

Still wearing the skins of Judith?

95

He discovered later that he actually wanted what he tried to get.

96

Aesthetic (i.e., formal) decisions, not for aesthetic (i.e., taste) reasons.

97

Why do you adopt the values of the community that rejects you?

98

He can't help regretting missed chances to have said something impressive or self-important—about his knowledge of foreign languages, for instance.

99

Why, in her presence, do we become overly protective of what we know, when she is ready to share all her knowledge with us and learn from us?

100

Those three numbers made him smile wistfully.

101

He mopes in her presence; this moping angers her.
—Both are absolutely correct.
But not natural.

102

She can't talk to me and thinks I'm doing it to her and maybe it's true.

103

Enunciating as if responding to a question in an examination. As if being examined.

104

Your gestures have changed.
The wave not as open.
Which is the fundamental feature of a wave.

105

I know all about being nervous.

106

Critics learn about life primarily through criticism, which is part of life.

107

He has an unfair advantage in that his subject is inherently interesting.

108

He made up his mind approximately two years later.

109

Never allow yourself to articulate your motives.

110

"I am not happy," he said proudly.

111

Which lie did he tell to explain his presence here?

112

Aren't we going to pretend that we didn't hear it?

113

What do mistakes and endings look like with people?

114

I can put this word anywhere I want.

Example of artistry.

115

I know myself poorly.

—That is what indecisive means. Making poor decisions.

116

Getting up and moving around will not help right now.

Being awake will not help.

Sitting up won't help.

Turning on a light won't help.

117

Surprised at my presence here. And wondering how I tricked myself into it?

118

I would do it "in a second" (immediately)
I will do it "in a second" (reluctantly)

119

And I ate the strange candy in the mini-bar.

120

Filing is about forgetting not remembering.
Not so that you can put your hands on it easily but so that you won't suddenly be staring at it.
How many mnemonic devices have the same function.

121

I need to talk to someone while eating; otherwise I eat too quickly.

122

My brain made a decision that it now regrets, and it punishes itself by going over the decision exhaustively.
Any new information is a signal to renew the process.
The result of the process is always that the original decision was wrong.
The only possible conclusion, because no advantage could make up for the pain of the process.

123

You evaded the questions brilliantly.

124

It keeps you awake at night and it wakes you up in the morning.

125

Why was this the right decision, I sometimes ask myself hopefully.

126

You have to schedule him.
Because he will be sure to fill completely whatever time you give him.

127

"it made sense"
It did not make sense; it made him unhappy.

128

Complicate your life as therapy.

129

The train and I are both getting up.
And yawning.

130

Shocked by his own action.
He had not yet rationalized it to himself.

131

Possible functions of a justice system:
welcoming
forgiveness

132

Because I prefer the product sold in video stores to the product sold in bookstores.
(Not because I prefer videos to books, but the books I like do not sell.)

133

It is called "defense."

134

It's safe not to pay attention to what they are saying.

135

"I suspect"—his frame.
The frame of his speech is suspicion.

136

Reading warms a room.

137
He makes women suffer instead of art.
He would make art objects suffer if he could not find a substitute.

138
We perform these rituals to protect the rest of the world from our god.

139
I get nervous just being around your job and responsibilities.

140
These doodads just make things difficult to repair.
These colored lights are just something else that can break down and have to be repaired.

141
Does it look like the signature of an adult?
What is that middle initial doing?

142
Part of your job as an animal is being hunted; another part is running away.

143
Tonight you will not escape this conversation.

The world cup for boredom

[November 2005-May 2006]

1

just the burden of
extreme love

2

Stuck in the same present tense as all painting and literature.

3

Or something like a sandwich.

4

Velcro coming away from itself.

5

At least she's making something.
At least you're paying attention to the words that are drawn to it.

6

He doesn't go looking for them.
He's a magnet for them.
The space around his shape is increasingly cluttered with insulting images of himself.

7

No one can tell what he wants, least of all himself.
They assume it's the opposite of what they want.

8

The magisterial presence chose not to be a good influence.

9

My friend Jane likes to say that she has no friends.
Is this a way of telling me that we are not friends.
Is she asking me not to treat her as friend.

10

Hold onto that tiredness. You may want it later.

11

He identifies the weakest one* and dominates that one.
(i.e., he is not interested in:
mutuality, or
a challenge.)
*the one he takes to be weakest

12

The anthropologist's solution.
—Add culture.
—You are missing culture.
—Even television would be sufficient.

13

Maybe those are two names (inventive, decisive) for a single quality that I can't identify and which I lack.

14

Everyone predicted that I was going to do the opposite of what they wanted.

15

A drawer full of questions.

16

My present circumstances are my enemy.
—False. Everything else (your past circumstances, your future, the life you imagine in other places and from different decisions) injures you, makes you suffer, and is your enemy.
Ideally a person should be your enemy, because you can defeat a person.

17

she can quote
the suicide note

18

Books are important, but you are more important.
You shouldn't feel jealous of books.
I don't give food to books.

19

Confusion on occasions when he is eating or sipping tea and reading—is he feeding the book?

He must have something to read for as long as he is eating.

20

Ancient emotional material for poems.

21

Sudden changes in pressure registered by the expanding and contracting lines.

22

He struck a vein of clear thinking and articulate speech.

23

He can't resist giving himself the compliment.

"I only give it to people I like."

24

Maternity is the condition of having absolute power over another creature.

25

He let his beard grow to seem less human.

26

The smell on your hand.
The greasy spicy smell on your hand.
On your hand and in the hall and on the street.
(particular and overdetermined)

27

A degree of calculation that seems incompatible with sincere feeling.

28

He pauses to consider the implications of the fact that he is able to read any poem.

29

How difficult it is to describe you in a poem without making you look like a king, or speak in a poem without sounding like a king.

30

The problem, which he calls majesty, of being visible like kings.

31

Act in the sense of pretending, and in the sense of doing.

32

The bed breathing under your back.

33

The sound of his dinner in the other room, before it joined him.

34

They went out with boys they didn't care for because they liked each other so much.
Each frequently abused the other's boyfriend (but not in her company).
They were allowed to abuse each other's boyfriends except when they were together.
It would have been inappropriate to abuse her own.

35

Getting off the plane he felt his brain waking up.
He realized:
that it had been sleeping on the plane
that previously it had been asleep for a week or longer

36

"You seem to shake your head and laugh to yourself a lot."

37

Everything makes me laugh and think.
But not in California.

38

Smug, condescending, paternalistic, enlightened relaxation.

39

The portrait of a student resembles the body of her teacher, although student and teacher are distinct physical types.

40

He immediately starts doing dishes.

41

And I washed what I thought was mine.

42

Whether he really liked what he believed he liked, and what he believed.

43

She was the only one who wouldn't ruin it for him.

44

Obviously people have tails.

45

I wish you wouldn't have anything to do with that sponge.

46

"I'm doing all right," i.e., all right because you are doing something.

47

You just want to eat my books.
—I would eat them all if I could.

48

If you don't cut it into slices, no one will take a piece.

49

I enjoy watching other people eat and read equally.

50

Sounds like games to me, doesn't sound like fun.

51

The microexpression of fear that everyone recognized because they had never seen it before.

52

Now he has learned to close his eyes when someone reads poetry.
If he could close his ears he would do that too.

53

What if my brain could crawl around alone and unprotected, without dragging the rest of me with it?

54

For some, it's easier to have others do the work for you; for some, it's easier to do the work yourself.

55

Some questions have no honest answer.

56

Her letter was convincing for those who didn't know anything about its subject.

57

Internal and external drives, like on a personal computer.

58

This one is trying to look stern, while another is trying to look amused.

59

"I may never get another opportunity to prove that I have a sense of humor."

60

The name on his lips is not the one circulating in his thoughts.
An expression of uncuriosity.

61

This one is trying on a skin.

62

Forming or falling away from form?

63

He expects a W-2 from his ex-girlfriend.
Breaking away from form.

64

Uses his own name as a swear word.
The creature takes its own name in vain.

65

We can cause anxiety.
That is something we can do.
A form of manipulation that works.

66

He started going to museums and now he is in one.

67

How do you collect and sort information.
I do not need to ask where you store it.

68

I thank people every day for things I do not want.
Every single day I ask for things I do not want.

69

"I envy no one"—false.
"I envy an entire country."

70

Someone that intelligent can't possibly be such a bastard. Can he?

71

How difficult it is to spell crystal!

72

He put it off because he thought it would be easy to do later; on later occasions he found he was too embarrassed to do it.

73

When I get a hearing aid, I don't want it to be flesh-colored, at least not the color of my flesh.

74

He pronounced “question” as a three-syllable word.
Add a syllable to question.

75

He put a space, an escape hatch, in the middle of every sentence.

76

Humility can’t be authenticated.

77

Pen drops to floor (from pocket).
Bottle top drops to floor (from hand).

78

Food without text.

79

Inorganic gossip (e.g., in a book, newspaper, or magazine).

80

No living poet can explain the difference between lay and lie.
Not even Jennifer uses them correctly.

81

It’s so obvious they have to pretend they already know it.

82

So must all things be recorded, so that you don't ever find them without looking for them.

83

The illusion of currency which is only mediocrity.

84

"unforgivable" (dream word, recovered with effort)
Awake with worry covering an angry dream.

85

Disappointing? "Unforgivable!"

86

He is invited to dance and responds by removing pen and notebook from his pockets.

87

Your late entrance is more remarkable than your absence would have been.

88

I believe that I am a loving person, but I do not respond to inappropriate demands for love from gods, nations, schools, works of art, or people.

89

Tacit refusal, and (more surprising) direct refusal.

When asked, he still said no.

He continued to say no.

He mouthed the word no.

He pronounced it.

90

Wrong to assume that laughter and amusement exclude arousal.

91

Maybe most people lie all the time.

Maybe I do—no one notices until I'm in a position where my words are recorded and repeated.

92

If you asked me to design a person, it might turn out like that.

I might subtract the self-loathing and add an emotional memory.

93

"If you asked me to design a person"—not someone for me to be attracted to, just a good example of a person.

"I'm not trying to design a girlfriend, just a person."

"And I would recommend her to anyone as a girlfriend, but I would never go for a second swim in those raging waters."

94
Dream: carrying the cat around at the library.

95
Does one side make false statements about the other side.

96
If there isn't a person who wants me there, if someone doesn't say, addressing me directly, that she would be pleased to see me there, then the feeling of necessity (that my attendance at the event is necessary) is only paranoia or projection, and really it is a question for my pleasure and conscience only.

97
Does thinking cause problems?

98
When you put me on display, you also put my responses and moments of inattention on display.

99
How much of our intellectual work is reciting lists of names?

100
The problem of remembering what you like.
Not many people are able to recite their list.
Even I have forgotten when asked.

101

The second time it becomes law.
It only needs to happen twice.

102

They liked it because they were interested.

103

One advantage of not being unionized is that we don't have to attend any meetings.

104

No one wants to be the standard.
We use "standard" to describe what we are not doing.

105

I believe you feel guilty about your behavior toward me and are avoiding me. This explanation is both a compliment to me and consistent with my own patterns of motive and behavior.

106

For a moment, as you're falling, pure lyricism, a gesture that has no purpose.

107

Paternal? Avuncular!
A world of uncles and nephews.

108

He said uncertainly that he loved me.

109

People are not symmetrical.

110

The hand that isn't writing gets tired first: from the other part of writing, supporting the notebook.

111

Why read a book when I can read your mind?

112

"Marxists should never eat human flesh"—but you can eat human flesh and follow the laws of the market.

113

How well can one see through those partly transparent curtains?

114

The typical defense that the office does not need tidying because "you know where things are," which is really saying that the system is not adaptable.
And fear of accidental discovery, which will occur in the event of reorganization.

115

They have to come up with a different answer the second time, to justify meeting twice.

116

His method makes it easy to collect materials for poems, but not to assemble them.
His method keeps the materials separate.
His method *is* to separate the materials.

117

Because they appear in the same order every time?
Because they are *only* arranged in order—they never cross?

118

Is it better to feel better?

119

Are you a creature that doesn't like its own ways? Then you have already committed suicide.

120

One of the most powerful rhetorical moves that can be made: "That's not what you said you wanted last week."
—Yeah, I changed my mind. Last week I wanted one thing; this week I want something else.

121

Almost as good: "That's not what I just said."

—Of course it isn't; it's a paraphrase, an interpretation, of what you just said. How can you expect your sayings to have any power or value if no one can paraphrase them?

122

I think I am homesick?

But where is my home?

123

It isn't easier to remain as you are. You have to keep working at it.

124

How far do you have to go inside your body to find something that feels good?

125

Sort of a relief not to dream about you, as I have been doing for the past two weeks. Unless the point of the dream is that I am trying to imitate you?

126

It is surprising that I know you well enough to put you in a dream, that you left enough of an impression on me to return in a dream.

127

I am a literalist, so I live in a world in which there are no puns.
This is a place in which it is difficult for me to be an adult.

128

They need punishment.
They crave punishment.
And babytalk.

Journal of pleasant studies

[June-September 2006]

1

Thank you for allowing me to grasp the laws of this country.

2

"Yes, I'd like to buy some social ties, please?"

3

People who come to me for advice should expect ambivalence.

4

Take as much as you can, whether you want it or not.

5

Almost no one has the same behavior inside and outside of the family.

6

How to write books so that they are about what they say they are about.

7

Most of what we know about the secret practices of Greek religions is derived from polemics against paganism by the fathers of the Christian church.
The usefulness of unsympathetic descriptions.

8

An unusual case of paralysis due to overproduction.
Reasons for overproduction: lack of support; unfortunate sensitivity to criticism.

9

I should have defended her against an unrecognizable description that may have been an attempt to gratify me.
Did he calculate that I would want to hear a bad description?
Then I should have corrected him.

10

One of her personal rules was that the landlord should not be able to see her boyfriend.

11

Something about me generalized.
Something about me said in a way that did not have to be about me.

12

You are not someone who acts or does not act out of guilt.

13

I am a literalist, which means that I do not know how to interpret figurative language.

I do not recognize it? I think it is effective? I think it should be taken seriously? In any case, I interpret as literally as possible.
"I always believe your whoppers," your exaggerations and puns.

14

Games = play + aggression
Two qualities that I lack, refuse, or misrecognize.

15

"You took me in"
=
internalized, protected, fooled
The umbrella term would be confidence.
All the meanings of confidence.

16

Your exit makes a path for me to follow.

17

First you mentioned something that I had to talk about, then I mentioned something that I had to talk about; I couldn't leave without talking about them.
I can go when no one is saying anything that needs to be talked about.

18

Difficult to talk about these things (books) when you're inside them.

19

"We broke up." Even these divisions are, however reluctantly, symmetrical.

20

When someone says respect, it usually translates as its opposite.

21

He doesn't want to name things or put them in order.
What about dividing them?

22

The wedding is designed to protect them from each other.

23

"Louder!"
"I'm sorry, you'll just have to listen harder."

24

They had no way of being together in public.
They never figured out what to do with one more person.

25

The entire city is colored by this problem (person).

26

There is no such thing as literary fame.
It means being studied in school.

27

Repair the broken ones and send them into battle.
Put the pieces into person molds and send them back to the playing field.

28

Do we applaud?
—No. It was not an aesthetic experience.

29

If you can play with your camera, then I can play with my notebook.
When I look down I'm taking his picture.

30

I am embarrassed by this intimacy which I am supposed to witness—the purpose of the event is for me to witness it.

31

Every one of your traits, everything good and bad, has now been revealed.

32

Lyricism: things are happening that do not have to happen, on which survival does not depend.

33

I am not playful but I do like to laugh.
I am so mature that I will laugh at anything!

34

Guilty, bored, annoyed, angry, or maybe just embarrassed—by the way it started or ended? And the middle?

35

Shouldn't each element in the series have a possessive form?

36

Whoever makes her happiest longest is luckiest.

37

"Stop it," he cried happily.

38

They have the impression that it explains their world, but it merely explains them.

39

It's an insult to be evicted from a property because it has a newly-discovered historical significance.
"These ancient artifacts are more important than you."
"Get out so that these dead things can live here."

40

The rules are so complicated I have had to develop ways of making them irrelevant.

41

I have never been threatened by the idea of solitary confinement, but maybe no one is.

42

Why not trick the world into believing you are decent people?

43

Are you eating to avoid talking to me?
She accuses him of eating to keep from talking.

44

Why not try to get your neighbors to like you?
In politics, they don't even need to really like you; all you have to do is give them a reason to pretend to like you.

45

She likes the parts of your body that smell strongest best.

46

His problem is that he can only hurt people when he's angry.

47

The only one who can appreciate you is the one who knows the whole sad story.
Who knows you are a carrier.

48

Delay means they are looking for a reason not to do it, and they will find one, and it will not happen.

49

Two shy people are being uncharacteristically aggressive toward each other.
I have identified a new form of awkwardness!

50

Is there a more positive word than yes?

51

A more exciting word than yes.
A luckier word than yes.

52

The class of people who wink.

53

I now believe interest is a delicate thing that can easily be destroyed.

54

By the time the critic arrives on the scene, most of the work has been done.

55

She wants to attack every object that you bring into the apartment.

56

Several quiet hours to themselves where their consciousnesses do not overlap.

57

What is so great about having a body?
If a body doesn't even have color?

58

He supported me in ways that did not help—for example, by lying to me.

59

I am like a tree; I create shade for myself.

60

Boxes in my living room:

—CONTROL YOUR DESTINY

—STRUGGLE FOR ACCOUNTABILITY

—AMERICAN: BEYOND OUR GRANDEST NOTIONS

61

Leading a child or a suitcase.

62

I always want to hold on to the item that has been refused, and to retain both items that have been shown to be incompatible.

63

He could have solved most of his problems by eating a nutritious lunch every day.

64

Thus I have sacrificed a lot for a clarity I do not even fully possess.

65

Between finishing breakfast and going out the door I lose fifteen minutes in which nothing happens except brushing my teeth and tying my shoes.

66

And your yawns are splitting your head.

67

Isn't there a way to make that argument without pissing people off?

68

So your plan is to teach them by humiliating them in front of the school?

69

They don't want you to remind them that they lied to you.

70

You have made me very sick.
I mean proud.

71

She says "perceive you" because she does not want to privilege one sense over the others.
Even the senses for which we do not have names.
Even senses that have no organs.

72

He lives in a world in which there is almost no good poetry.

73

If he is right, there is no reason to care about anything.

74

Motto: PERFECT IN PARTS.

75

People like me shouldn't drive cars or have kids.

76

An expression of modesty (when self-directed) becomes an expression of skepticism (when directed at others).
The word is "attempt."

77

How ineffectually I inhabit this city!

78

Does it still count as sex if someone dies?

79

"We didn't sleep together, but she did eat some of the bread, and which is really more intimate?"

Merciless fun

[October-December 2006]

1

The brushing of two solipsisms and the surfaces of their wobbly containers.

2

Even when he was in an agony of feeling, you read more into him than there was.

3

We have many things in common but they are not complementary.

4

much as I endeavor not to hate myself
I would not want to date myself

5

Jumping. To escape an unbearable situation he had created.

6

Doing and making are sort of the same.

7

How do you take (handle) rejection?
Of course your own rejection can be fatal (to yourself as well as another).

8

By personal choice, by physical necessity, and on principle.

9

Imagine a country where no one had a sense of humor.

10

Now and then you get a glimpse of his life from outside, and how lightly and poorly he inhabits it.

11

Along with trade secrets, we learn affectations.

12

But he has already chosen his books and can only say what they say. It's what he wanted to say when he chose them.

13

Someone always wants to know how you became an artist. It's an interesting question, because what is the answer? When it is not an option given to you in childhood or school. They are asking for your bildungsroman.

14

Coffee, tea, chocolate.
To fool you into thinking that you had a hot meal.

15

Wouldn't it be interesting to be gifted with her gifts? Fortunately she writes books and articles to make us aware of her awareness.

16

"I don't read books; I'm a literary critic."

17

I am in the business of staring at things.

18

The impact of awkward is similar to intimidating.

19

"Whom I respect"—if by respect he means "I will always offer the worst possible description of her actions" and "I will always assign her bad motives."

20

You look sorry when you climax.
Or some other word.

21

Easy to find a word for the expression, but what is the word for the event?

22

You won't recognize it as your shape, no matter how clearly I say it.

23

Caressing or measuring, which is more intimate?

24

Divide the remainder into Friday, Saturday, Sunday.

25

He is talking again.
(1.5 hours later)

26

Drifting off to sleep, in a sort of dream, I suddenly understood that the first-person singular was a nickel, and all the pronouns, all the speaker positions, correspond to coins. Words do not represent things; they indicate a range of values, and they circulate.

27

His secret is wordplay.
His secret love.
"I love to speak its name."

28

Even those who know better believe *The New York Times.*

29

A way of withdrawing that translates as coolness—unlike mine, which translates as awkwardness.

30

You should walk out when it goes that badly, when it starts to go bad, when you feel that slow and stupid.
—No, that would be too easy. You have to do your job, which is to remain in the room, even while it goes badly.

31

He is a baby. He is all the things men call each other because they are afraid of being thought weak.

32

We want to require, ensure, and confirm that everyone has the same problems.

33

What you have in common is cluelessness, not manhood.

34

Time is easy.
Time will take it from anyone who will give it.

35

A kind of roteness to all my learning.

36

That was very brave (to ask, or come close to asking, for an invitation), so it would be impolite not to offer.

37

He used to invent problems that couldn't be solved. Then he became one.

38

No more than I'm interested in being friends with everybody.

39

"I have to run."
She actually ran.

40

He experienced a slip between the cup and the lip, or the cup experienced it.

41

You say what you think you have done because you have not really done it.
You have not accomplished it.
Or: the task is not complete until you describe it.

42

The RESPECT card didn't have my name on it. It just said RESPECT.

43

When one is happy, one wakes up early.

44

How many hours I have spent writing gracious notes that I do not send!
Or notes that attempt to be gracious.

45

I examined my motives, saw that they were not good; so I didn't look.

46

She speaks with absolute confidence; he rejects her with absolute certainty.
I have played the same scene without the confidence and certainty.

47

Up early to steal the neighbor's newspaper.

48

We are only beginning to discover the truth of the observation that people have tails.

49

At the halfway point, she asked if everything was all right.

50

Cleaning destroys.
Cleaning does not preserve.
"Housework must fail" for there to be a house.

51

It would be nice to see you, and nicer not to.

52

We all have those fits of feeling and do not voice them.
Even I am as sad as that once or twice an hour.
Sad as a wailing baby.

53

Less and less, I regret occasions when I am unable to make up answers.

54

He looks like you, but his name is me, I mean mine.

55

Can you hear my voice? That proves you're a special person.

The better fabricator

[January-March 2007]

1

I never told you, because I am not the personality who has the disease.

2

Like me, he is a worrywart.
He does not know "what the sweetness of living is."
A vampiric, miserly way of having pleasure.

3

I think about it only enough to act and explain my actions, not enough for you to act, not enough to explain how you act.

4

Edges of her mouth are working as though about to speak, smile, grimace, or bite.

5

Discretion (irony).
What if the critics did appreciate the irony, but they were too polite to mention it?

6

Her mother is a dipshit.
She can't say it.
Her friend can't say it.
(She won't allow her friend to say it, because they're talking about her mother.)

Even I can't say it.

The critics can't say it? Here discretion breaks down. (The critics are dipshits?)

7

I always get one yes and one no.

Maybe that's not a fact about me, maybe that's what people are like: some accept things, some reject them.

8

Between noon and four I might actually take a position.

9

Before noon you could probably get me to support any agenda—vocally, if not in writing.

10

Both she and I derive things from him, but he, the original, carries them with a better grace.

11

What if he finds a god that he has not worshipped?

What if he doesn't know how to worship this god?

12

Advertisement: BECOME A PRIVATE MERCENARY!

13

Her large hands quickly (gently) are pressing the keys.

14

A false coherence. Falsely together.
They have false problems that they create themselves and fix quickly, when they feel like it, as though understanding that they never should have existed.

15

If they blame one another, there's no hope for them.
If they try to defend what they did to her, or make excuses for their behavior, *or blame her for it*, then they are not worth a moment's consideration, they are not worth it.
If they say anything other than that they misbehaved and thereby lost her, then there's no hope for them.

16

Unfit for the world.
Unfit for anything else.

17

He takes, and he is not grateful.

18

That is to say, we are not friends, but we are connected by a mutual friend.

19

Others use tools, others make reasoned arguments, others have language; only this creature wears a garment.

20

That's not a definition of art, that's an example of something that isn't art.

21

Sometimes you have to formulate a question just to stay awake.

22

The point of the battle of Thermopylae is not superior tactics against greater numbers. The prohibition against retreat means that the Spartans have no other tactical options.

23

The point of the battle of Thermopylae is that one could not possibly identify with the Spartans.

I can be a Spartan only by giving up everything that I value.

Spartans are admirable, but they have no culture, history, literature, etc.

They do not know "what the sweetness of living is."

They are admirable only in one way.

24

"none to speak of"

=

nothing that will sustain the pressure of speech
nothing that would not be injured by a long discussion, or just by telling

25

To be rejected by someone who knows you that intimately, who appreciates the qualities you really have, who has enjoyed every part of you that can be enjoyed, would hurt.

26

It seems that I was half-awake the entire time.
And I came to just as it was ending.

27

Suddenly her hair was gathered in a braid.

28

I was kind of damaged.
And I put myself together too hastily.
I didn't match anyone else's tabs and notches.

29

I can't stand art that asks me to participate.
"Do your job."
"Finish making it before you give it to me."

30

They can't even survive on your blood, but they can make you miserable.

31

The operatives were not aware that there was such a thing as institutional oversight, until they were tested.

32

"We will reimburse you for any cost you incur in notifying us of the errant communication."

33

These simple people make aggressive jokes when they are nervous.

34

They try to defuse awkwardness by calling it awkward.
An awkward acknowledgment.

35

An unequal partnership.

He's here to be in school; she's here to be with him. She can equalize the division somewhat by teasing me. She takes something from me that he can't have, because I am his teacher.

And she is lonely. And bored. And curious.

36

It helps her to know someone he can't really know but respects, so that she can disrespect him.

37

They know it's the funniest thing they can say; they use it sparingly.

38

Do the most advanced work at the most elementary level.

39

And she drank one of the free samples—rapidly.

40

He only made one mistake.

He made exactly one mistake (to prove that he could make one).

41

Then perhaps it wasn't a mistake, because he learned something.

42

Throw yourself into it completely, to remember it has almost no value.

43

Not rational, but predictable.
He chooses his own death, because it comes with a desk lamp with his name on it.

44

I am able to predict what you will say, but I am not able to say it.
I can predict but not explain.

45

I am trying to look as though I care about my appearance, and I am also trying not to care.

46

A very sad man gets a haircut.

47

I am about as much of a misanthrope as you are a coquette.

48

He turns the page without reading.

49

Separate normal from natural—which you do anyway in separating society from nature.

50

Make the bed, or you might just fall back into it.

51

Part of it was seeing him want it, and not get it, and have to pay for it; part of it was seeing her want it and get it.
Because I am both of them.
That's why I want what she got.

52

You say you are wondering, which is a lie.
You ask for clarification because you are certain.
You ask me to clarify, that is, to expose myself.

53

By instinct they find the nourishment they need.

Aaron Kunin is a poet, critic, and novelist. He is the author of two books of poems, *Folding Ruler Star* and *The Sore Throat and Other Poems*, and a novel, *The Mandarin*. He lives in Los Angeles.

LETTER MACHINE EDITIONS

Anselm Berrigan, *To Hell With Sleep*

Edmund Berrigan, *Can It!*

Peter Gizzi, *Ode: Salute to the New York School*

Aaron Kunin, *Grace Period: Notebooks, 1998-2007*

Juliana Leslie, *More Radiant Signal*

Farid Matuk, *This Isa Nice Neighborhood*

Fred Moten, *the feel trio*

Sawako Nakayasu, *Texture Notes*

Travis Nichols, *Iowa*

Andrea Rexilius, *Half of What They Carried Flew Away*

Sara Veglahn, *Another Random Heart*

John Yau, *Exhibits*